THE GOD HUNT

The Delightful Chase and

the Wonder of Being Found

KAREN MAINS

InterVarsity Press
Downers Grove, Illinois

InterVarsity Press
P.O. Box 1400, Downers Grove, IL 60515-1426
World Wide Web: www.ivpress.com
E-mail: mail@ivpress.com

InterVarsity Press® *is the book-publishing division of InterVarsity Christian Fellowship/USA*®*, a student movement active on campus at hundreds of universities, colleges and schools of nursing in the United States of America, and a member movement of the International Fellowship of Evangelical Students. For information about local and regional activities, write Public Relations Dept., InterVarsity Christian Fellowship/USA, 6400 Schroeder Rd., P.O. Box 7895, Madison, WI 53707-7895, or visit the IVCF website at <www.ivcf.org>.*

All Scripture quotations, unless otherwise indicated, are taken from the Holy Bible, New International Version®. NIV®. *Copyright ©1973, 1978, 1984 by International Bible Society. Used by permission of Zondervan Publishing House. All rights reserved.*

Jaroslav Vajda's hymn "God of the Sparrow, God of the Whale," in Dorothy Bass, Practicing Our Faith *©1997 by Dorothy Bass, is used by permission of John Wiley & Sons, Inc.*

"Sharon's Christmas Prayer" from The Hour of the Unexpected, *©1977, 1992 by John Shea, used by permission of the author.*

Every effort has been made to trace and contact copyright holders for additional materials quoted in this book. The author will be pleased to rectify any omissions in future editions if notified by copyright holders.

Cover design: Cindy Kiple

Cover image: Karen Huntt Mason/Getty Images

ISBN 0-8308-3241-6

Printed in the United States of America ∞

Library of Congress Cataloging-in-Publication Data

Mains, Karen Burton.
  The God hunt: the delightful chase & the wonder of being found/
Karen Mains.
     p. cm.
Includes bibliographical references.
 ISBN 0-8308-3241-6 (alk. paper)
 1. Christian life. 2. Desire for God. 3. Presence of God I.
 Title
BV4509.5.M256 2003
248.4—dc21

                                                                2003006794

P	17	16	15	14	13	12	11	10	9	8	7	6	5	4	3	2	1
Y	15	14	13	12	11	10	09	08	07	06	05	04	03				

TO DOUG AND SHARON WORDEN

Many times you have secured

our very survival.

In you we have seen

God's compassionate concern.

Contents

1 Hide-and-Seek 9

2 Wonder 25

3 Going the Wrong Way to Buffalo 39

4 The Thrill of the Hunt 60

5 Trail Signs 81

6 Sightline 97

7 Hunting Gear and Master Hunters 110

8 Keeping a Life List 127

9 Every Season Is Hunting Season 145

10 Walking in a Hero's Shoes 163

11 Gathering Day 178

Further Reading 190

I

HIDE-AND-SEEK

*I am constantly struck by the proximity of "play" and "pray";
this is brought home to me in serendipitous messages
from my word processor, when my fingers take on a life
of their own and I find myself writing,
"It will be necessary to play about this."*

MARGARET GUENTHER

Who has never played hide-and-seek? I've yet to find one person, and I've inquired of people all over the world, in a variety of cultural and geographical settings, even of those born with severe physical limitations. We all remember the delight of seeking or of being found, and this universal game is an apt paradigm for that lifelong quest, the spiritual hunt. The passion children bring to hide-and-seek is the same passion we need to bring to finding God.

In case your recall of childhood is dim, let me refresh your memory. The game begins with one player who is "It." It chooses a spot that serves as home base. She closes her eyes and starts counting to a determined number. The game begins as the other players race to find hiding spots, and when the determined number has been called out, It then shouts, "Ready or not, here I come!" It attempts to search out the hiders and tag them before they can reach home base. If the hiders reach home base and are not tagged, they are safe; if they are tagged, they are out. Hiders

can run for home base without being found first by It. The player
who is tagged is It in the next round.

Of course, there are endless variations of the basic form of
hide-and-seek. One of my favorites is Capture the Flag, which I
played as a child in the dark with 15-20 players on each team at a
campsite that was large enough for real hiding—a more sophisticated approach, certainly, but basically hide-and-seek.

Everyone—even the smallest child, such as our granddaughter
Joscelyn—can play hide-and-seek. As a two-year-old, Josie called
the game, "Gotcha!" An adult (or a teen pressed into action as
babysitter) hid (in obvious ways), and the little girl went seeking
and found her prey. This brought on wild gales of enchanted
laughter, delicious toddler gurgles, as she cried out, "Gotcha!"

Go back in memory; play again the game of hide-and-seek.
Pretend you are the one who is hiding. Can you recall the favorite
places you used to hide? Do you remember those secret spots
where no one would think of looking for you? Was it beneath the
basement stairs? Or high in the apple tree? Under the kitchen
sink? On the top shelf of a closet behind storage boxes? In the
woods? In the barn? In a city alley?

Now remember what it was like to be so still that not a breath,
not a cough, not a movement would reveal your hiding place.
Even your lungs, the inhaling and exhaling, seemed to slow. You
were keenly aware, every cell of your body watching for the
hunter who was hunting you. You were in a suspended state of
sustained anticipation.

Now recall what it was like to be the hunter. Every nerve-
ending in your body is on alert. Your eyes scan the field of the
hunt. Did you see a brief movement? Your ears are pitched to a
heightened level of awareness. Did you hear a muffled giggle? Did
someone breathe quickly, or bump a shelter? You inch closer and

closer, watching for any who might make a dash for home base. You also are in a suspended state of sustained anticipation.

This is what it can be like to hunt for God. The concept of hunting and finding has great power to evoke longing, emotions, particular understandings, even compulsive activity in all of humankind, no matter the age or intelligence. The aptitude for hunting for and finding God is native to every human heart, but as we mature we often lose or neglect the capacity to do so. We only become intent on finding him when terror is nearby, when sadness insists on keeping company, or when pain becomes a relentless stalker. Let us instead begin the God Hunt as a game of hide-and-seek—in a childlike way, with laughter and delight.

What is the God Hunt? Simply defined, the God Hunt is choosing to recognize God anytime he intervenes in our everyday life. It is a tool my husband and I developed decades ago to teach our four children how to experience the presence of God in their everyday activities. We firmly believe that it is a sin to make the Christian life boring or theoretical (it is neither). In developing spiritual disciplines, or in teaching holy truth, we attempt to apply this teaching model: *What is learned with pleasure is learned full measure.* The God Hunt, because of its playful quality, has been used by hundreds of thousands of seekers worldwide, people who have desired to identify God in their everyday lives but have had difficulty in doing so. Good teachers encourage play. The German poet-philosopher Friedrich Schiller wisely suggested that human beings are completely human only at play.

Scripture teaches that God is an active and communicative being, one who is present in his creation, ready to come to the aid of those who love him and eager to be in constant communion. Look at the biblical evidence. The men and women who discovered God were sheepherders, farmers, vinedressers, servant girls,

slaves, fishermen, tax collectors, town whores, the sick and the dying, the wealthy, kings and commanders, religious dignitaries, the
intelligentsia. No matter their status in life, they were all common
folk, everyday people like you and like me who had uncommon
encounters. The Almighty intervened in their ordinary rou-
tines—in the desert, in the field, in the garden, by the seashore,
along the river, in the town, at festivals and celebrations, during
high holy days, on the Sabbath. He is where his people are, joining
them in their daily lives.

Yet we moderns suffer from massive dissociative disorders—
split from ourselves, divided from one another, alienated (even
those of us who say we believe) from the God who loves us. Consequently we are filled with inexplicable longing to be unioned.
We attempt to reason our way back to connection, but this kind
of joining is best accomplished through the heart's way of knowing, through the experience of finding and through acquaintance.
The God Hunt, due to its playfulness, helps us find God in the ordinary events of living.

The God Hunt rules insist that participants take initiative to
seek after the Almighty, that we humans exercise intention and
look for him in the everyday, that we choose to seek him in the
commonplace. Often, however, we play the game of finding God
as though we were stumbling around in blind-man's bluff. We go
through the motions, bumbling and bumping, with a rag tied
around our spiritual eyes, and we learn to ignore the nudges and
pushes that are evidences of God participating in our everyday
worlds. We become benumbed, anesthetized.

At the end of his remarkable book *The Question of God: C. S. Lewis
and Sigmund Freud Debate God, Love, Sex, and the Meaning of Life,* Dr. Armand M. Nicholi Jr., professor at Harvard, closes this posthu-
mous dialogue between these two great minds with a quote that

summarizes Lewis's mature belief. "We may ignore, but we can nowhere evade, the presence of God. The world is crowded with Him. He walks everywhere incognito. And the incognito is not always easy to penetrate. The real labor is to remember to attend. In fact to come awake. Still more to remain awake."

Finding God incognito in the world is not a ho-hum proposition. It is delight. It is joy. It is wonder. It is a childlike wiggling anticipation that somewhere, any moment, just around the next corner, when you least expect it, the Divine is going to jump out, cry, "Boo!" and you are going to respond, "Gotcha!" This is wondrous, is it not?

LOOKING FOR GOD

There are four categories where we train people to look for God in their everyday lives. Of course, the capacities of an infinite God to interact with finite humanity are limitless. These four categories, however, are a helpful place for people to begin.

1. Any obvious answer to prayer

2. Any unexpected evidence of his care

3. Any help to do God's work in the world

4. Any unusual linkage or timing

A few illustrations from my prayer journal may be helpful. Although I can go back through thirty years of recorded God Hunt sightings, these samples are taken from the last month of my journal to make the point that having practiced this game/discipline for so long, I never—never—go through a day without finding ways God has intervened in my life.

Any obvious answer to prayer. A genetic high cholesterol level is something I've inherited from my lineage. My parents had high counts (when cholesterol was just beginning to be measured), as do my brother and sister. I have not been particularly careful about diet or exercise, but my brother is a dedicated runner, and in addition, he is healthily cautious about what he eats. Our levels are almost twin to each other! This is the sentence of genetically inherited high cholesterol; the counts can't be controlled through exercise or by a change in diet. (Craig and I are a case in point.)

Although I kept telling myself I needed to take this condition seriously, and I had been praying about the problem, it was my daughter who brought me to full attention. "Mother, you're a walking heart attack waiting to happen!" she said, not too delicately. (My "bad" cholesterol count was 329, to be exact.)

At this time a former employee contacted my husband, David, with news of a nutritional supplement that had almost miraculously reduced her symptoms from a complexity of distresses: fibromyalgia, multiple sclerosis and a host of other disabling conditions. I immediately was placed on the product—a high soy, high (high) fiber cocktail of nutrients, scientifically combined, shaken with water or juice and consumed three times a day. In five months my cholesterol count had dropped by one hundred points.

I would call this an obvious answer to prayer.

Any unexpected evidence of his care. We sent our son Joel overseas to India for two weeks on a video shoot (he is a director/producer/editor with our video team) for Gospel for Asia, a mission organization that calls out, trains and sends national missionaries throughout Asia. During this time David's father died, and although his death was imminent and Joel had fortunately had a chance to say his last goodbyes, it was still a stressful moment for us all to handle wakes, funerals, family gatherings, grave site ceremonies and the luncheon afterward.

On the morning of the funeral home visitation, I offered to take care of my grandson Elias John so my daughter-in-law Laurie could have a break from child-care and go to a beauty salon for an uninterrupted moment of private pampering. It wasn't long after Laurie had left my house that I received a frantic cell phone call. "Karen, I've had an automobile accident. The car is totaled."

You cannot imagine my anxiety or my dismay. I wasn't exactly sure where Laurie was or in what condition. I was stuck at home with a two-year-old and didn't have a car that morning, and my husband was in transit. I couldn't reach him, nor could I get through the automated phone system at our ministry to a live voice—all I could do was leave urgent voice mail messages. Frantically I dialed 911.

"My daughter-in-law has just called to say she's had an accident. I can hear the sirens. And please listen to me very carefully. My daughter-in-law is diabetic, and I don't know what effect this trauma will have on her insulin count."

"Hold on, lady," said the voice on the other end of the phone. "We're going to patch you into our dispatcher. We'll find her and talk you through this."

And indeed they did just that. In a little bit of time David got my frantic phone message, came hurtling home, drove up the street, found Laurie, dazed but undamaged (with just an airbag scrape under her chin), and the occupants in the other vehicle unharmed. He brought her home, and we tucked her in on the couch in front of the fireplace.

In a few moments a police officer knocked politely at our front door. He gently inquired of Laurie about the circumstances of the accident. Then he said to her, "Now please understand. None of us sets out to do this, to get banged up on the highway. This was an accident. That is why it is called an 'accident.'" This young man in his leather patrolman's jacket must have been a grad student in sensitivity training school. My jaw dropped, and tears came to my eyes. I escorted him to our front door. When he was outside, he asked in a very soft voice, "Now, is she going to be all right?"

Quietly my husband said, "Well, the car is totaled, but another millisecond and the passenger truck would have rammed into the driver's door; that could have been bad. Or what if Elias had been in the back seat? The other drivers were using a truck to move furniture and holding a toddler on their lap, without a seatbelt, in the front seat. What if the child had gone through the window?"

Laurie was safe. We weren't going to have a hospital incident on top of a funeral, or worse—a funeral on top of a funeral. Undeniably, we were convinced that we were surrounded by unexpected evidences of God's care.

Any help to do God's work in the world. I recently flew home from a ten-day trip overseas with one week to put the final details together for an Advent Retreat of Silence for thirty-some women. So much needed to be done, and even though our staff was in a highly busy space themselves, they assisted me in putting the final touches on the Advent Retreat with willingness, without complaint and with a spirit that brought great kindness and grace to my jet-lagging physiology.

Someone on the staff designed name cards (someone else found leftover name tags); another individual pulled a list of alphabetized names together, showing who had paid and who was rooming with whom. A check was totaled and funds transferred so I could pay the retreat center. Handouts were copied and collated; flyers were designed with coming events. Every time I turned around, another task was done. I went to the Advent Retreat with everything organized, no last-minute panic and with an hour or two to compose myself and get ready before the participants arrived. And yes, we all experienced a powerful time together waiting on God for the healing power of silence.

Unusual linkage or timing. One of my tasks at Mainstay Ministries is to write or gather the ideas for our monthly fund appeal. Since I have been raising funds for not-for-profit organizations since the age of eighteen, this frequently becomes a tiresome process for me. Some days I would give anything for someone to step into our organization, tap me on my shoulder and take this whole load off my back.

When I am putting a teaching ministry together, God frequently uses anything and everything to teach me. While developing a teaching program that used the metaphor of dance to show how to "step in time to God's sacred rhythms," it seemed as though all my spiritual reading, the conversations I had with friends, and the films, books and magazine articles from popular culture gave me examples of this concept. Even better, during this period of time I was the plenary speaker at a woman's conference where one of the workshops was being taught by a professor from a Christian college who was head of the dance minor. I attended, took copies of all her scriptural notes, and in a half-hour she had us all improvising worship dance. It was delightful!

However, I receive divine help from a heavenly Father who certainly understands that fundraising is not my gift, but is nonetheless a task I must do. Often when I have been working on a book or on a broadcast, God has provided the exact quote or the most fitting illustration in the very hour I was writing.

This December's year-end fund appeal began unintentionally

during a dinner table conversation among members of my Covenant Group. All six of us are involved in full-time ministry, and only
one (that I know of) has any real financial security for the future.
We were discussing the recent scandals of secular executive salaries
and retirement packages. At the time, the outrageous retirement
perks of Jack Welsh, former CEO of General Electric, were just being made public, not because there had been a disclosure to the
board of directors, but because his wife was demanding a fairer divorce settlement and the details were being revealed in court.

That same month I read the book *The Most Effective Organization
in the U.S.: Leadership Secrets of the Salvation Army.* In its pages I learned
how a two-billion-dollar transcontinental organization serves
thirty million customers with a dedicated workforce (including
its National Commander) that by secular standards is vastly over-
worked and underpaid.

A research visit to the Internet later, and suddenly a fund appeal idea came to mind: What was God thinking when he sent his
Son, who some might consider the CEO of the universe, into the
world in a state of poverty? Using the CEO scandals and the un-
certainty of the stock markets as points for contrast, I was able to
build a biblical Christmas letter reminding our donors of the
eternal securities in which they were really investing when they
supported Mainstay Ministries. God's timing was perfect!

A SERVANT'S ENCOUNTER WITH GOD

To further illustrate the four categories of the God Hunt, it is
helpful to turn to a delightful story from Scripture that demonstrates how one man found God in his everyday world. In Genesis
24 Abraham asks his chief servant to find a wife for his well-loved
son, Isaac. As if this task weren't difficult enough, the servant
must travel to Abraham's homeland, Mesopotamia, to find the

right woman. Read through the lens of humor, this story unfolds with charming insight.

"What if I find a wife, and the lady doesn't want to come with me?" the servant asks. This seems like an all too plausible scenario. What woman in her right mind would take off with a complete stranger, journey to a foreign land and marry a man she's never laid eyes on?

"He will send his angel before you," Abraham replies with almost childlike trust. Given the long faith-journey of Abraham's life, the servant knows that the direct intervention of God on his master's behalf is an unquestionable possibility. So he complies and obeys, perhaps resignedly, and arms himself with ten of his master's camels and loads of booty—choice gifts that are the signature of great wealth. Then the servant prays the inevitable O-God-help-me-how-did-I-get-into-this-dilemma prayer: "O LORD, God of my master Abraham, give me success today."

Obviously this is a ridiculous task. How in heaven's name is he going to choose a wife out of all the suitable women who live in Mesopotamia? Desperately he sets forth a proposition (he hopes this will make it easier): Whatever maiden he asks to give him a drink will also offer to water his camels. This is more than a lottery prayer request (whatever number comes up) but one that also reveals character—compassion, hospitality and initiative—on the part of whatever woman would consider watering the ten camels (count them) belonging to the stranger.

Wouldn't you know it, the very first woman out of the city gate happens to be beautiful, a virgin and an offspring from Abraham's own extended family? She readily gives the servant a drink to quench his thirst and volunteers to pour water into the trough for all the camels. (How about that? Gotcha!) Just imagine the steward's amazement.

Prudently the steward makes further arrangements. He asks to meet the family, inquiring of the young woman as to whether they have a place in their home where he might lodge. He meets her brother, Laban, and sister-in-law, Bethuel. He discovers the family tie. He tells his story about Abraham's mandate for an arranged marriage, and he recounts the evidence of divine intervention at the spring of water. He gives costly gifts to verify that he is telling the truth about his master's wealth. Rebekah's brother is open to the arrangement, but most wonderful, when given the choice as to whether she should wait ten days (as her relatives suggest in order to prepare for immigration) or leave right away, the young woman chooses to depart her home and family instantly. Talk about hide-and-seek, or better yet, finding and keeping.

Looking at this story, we can easily see God's presence in the everyday details of Abraham's servant's life and identify the four categories of the God Hunt.

Any obvious answer to prayer. Look at Abraham's servant. "O LORD, God of my master Abraham, give me success today," he prays, and God gives him astounding success. Finding Rebekah is an obvious answer to prayer.

Men and women often request help from God; he answers, and we forget. This is the normal pattern. But this is a petitioner who doesn't forget. In verse 26 we are told that he bows his head and worships: "Praise be to the LORD." He witnesses to God's intervention when he tells his story to Laban and Bethuel.

Any unexpected evidence of God's care. This story is filled with the quality of divine compassion. The old servant has traveled far, his master Abraham is near the end of his life, he has no idea where to start or how to begin to carry out his commission, and the very first young woman who comes to draw water from the spring is the wife of God's choosing for Isaac. How kind of God! How merciful that the wife hunt didn't take years and hundreds of interviews! Not only was the task quickly expedited, but what a find! The young woman is a virgin, beautiful, displays a willingness to work and to be helpful, and she believes the servant's story that God has directed his path. She sets herself with an eager readiness to be part of this drama on earth by immediately joining his caravan back to the waiting Isaac.

God's care is also displayed for Isaac. The Scriptures say, "Isaac brought her into the tent of his mother Sarah, and he married Rebekah. So she became his wife, and he loved her; and Isaac was comforted after his mother's death" (Genesis 24:67). One can only imagine Abraham's relief at having his promised son so successfully wedded.

Any help to do God's work in the world. Isaac's wife will be an important figure in the ongoing plan of God in building this peculiar nation he has chosen to love and use. The divine scheme is to create a lineage that will eventually provide bloodlines and an ancestral heritage for the birth of his Son, who is to bring redemption to the whole world. Abraham's servant could not possibly have foreseen the future implications of his faithful stewardship, but he was enabled by divine intervention to be a catalytic agent who would fulfill part of the grand master scheme. God was doing a work in time, and this man played a crucial role in that incredible history.

Unusual linkage and timing. What kind of master planning did it take for Abraham's servant to arrive outside the city of Nahor just as the women were coming out to draw water in the evening? What kind of arranging did it take for Rebekah to be the first to draw water at the well? In what ways had her heart been prepared? What sort of reputation did Abraham still have with his people that would allow her brother and sister-in-law to agree to this arranged marriage? How had wisdom been developed in the steward so he could plot an approach in this seemingly impossible scenario? How, through the years, had he developed such a faith in Abraham's God that he could trust that this same God would act on his behalf?

Linkage and timing are a set of occurrences that mesh together for our good in an amazing way and to which humans usually exclaim, "What a coincidence!" But it is not a coincidence; it is God working on our behalf. Linkage and timing often take years to develop and unfold, and we see an amazing example of it here in the pages of Genesis. It is not coincidence; it is God found in the God Hunt, that age-old delightful chase that always ends in the wonder of being found.

Sighting

Linda Richardson from Wheaton, Illinois, is a speech therapist, specializing in work with autistic children in the public school system. She tells of assisting a new five-year-old student, Wendy, to adjust to the unfamiliar environment of the classroom. How was this to be done since the child was without language? Linda and her colleagues devised a visual schedule that would lead Wendy through her day using pictures and symbols placed strategically on a chart. With this tool Wendy seemed to settle comfortably into the routine, that is, until her father came to pick her up at the end of the class.

At this time the little girl went into a frantic panic reaction. She kicked and screamed, and it took three adults to carry and place her in the family car. Through the years of working with autistic children, Linda has learned to follow the rule: Don't just do something; stand there. This is the opposite of the natural helping instinct: *Don't just stand there, do something. The quick reaction is often the wrong reaction for children with autism.*

What had caused this extreme behavior, and how could the child be helped? The teachers needed to stop, think empathetically, then get inside the child's mind and emotions. Linda, a devout Christian, and her professional team of colleagues devised one further symbol to cue the child about the end of class. On the visual schedule they pasted a picture of her father. When he pulled up outside the school to pick up his daughter, Wendy was shown the picture. Not only was there no kicking and screaming, Wendy would cry out, "Papa!" when her father arrived (despite the fact that most children with autism do not greet spontaneously). Then she walked to the car quietly and got in.

2

WONDER

A child in the cradle has the infinite in its eye.

VINCENT VAN GOGH

Let us begin the God Hunt with a childlike sense of wonder and with laughter. Christ himself said, "I tell you the truth, anyone who will not receive the kingdom of God like a little child will never enter it" (Luke 18:17). The Matthew version of this passage, rendered in another translation, reads, "Unless you turn and become like little children, you will never enter the kingdom of heaven" (Matthew 18:3 RSV). What does this mean? Does it mean we should suspend adult rationality (or at least suspend the compulsive rush to over-intellectualize our faith)? Does it mean we should forget the hard-won wisdom gained through lifelong experience (perhaps we don't know nearly as much as we think we know)? Is Christ chiding the too serious adults around him because they have lost their playful minds?

What exactly does the phrase "like a little child" imply? Certainly it has something to do with laughter. Laughter is one of the elements of childhood, an ability to participate in sacred hilarity; spontaneous celebrations of God with us are too infrequently experienced as we grow older.

Certainly children know one thing that most adults have forgotten, and that is how to play simply for the *fun* of it. Often there is no line between their work and play; neither duty nor ought-ness intrudes when they are concentrated and happy. Last winter on one Chicago day filled with sun-spangled snow, I hauled my grandchildren to the K-Mart and fitted them with boots and gloves, then stacked the station wagon high with borrowed sleds and turned all loose on the frozen and drifted golf course behind my daughter's house.

Sipping cocoa together, my daughter Melissa and I watched through the kitchen windows as the little ones pumped their legs back and forth up the steep hills, puffing away, then sliding down over and over for a blissful two hours. They came into the house for their own mugs of hot chocolate, cheeks rosy, laughing and breathless, full of stories, "Did you see us slide down the hill? Did you see us go two to a sled? Did you? Nathanael fell off. Did you see that?"

Work? Well, hardly, though it was work in a way. *Eutrapelia* is a better description, turning well, delighting in hardy play. "*Eutrapelia*," writes Tilden Edwards in his book *Sabbath Time*, "is an old, neglected human virtue identified by Aristotle that can lend understanding to the quality of authentic sabbath play. It derives from *eutrepo*, 'to turn well.' It is a virtue reflecting mobility of soul, one that is able to turn to lovely, bright, relaxing things without losing authentic self in them. It is a capacity to turn deeds or words into relaxation."

Mihaly Csikszentmihalyi, a psychologist and former chairman of the department of psychology at the University of Chicago, has been studying states of "optimal experience" for two decades. Optimal experiences are those moments when people are sus-pended in absolute concentration and are lost in their activity with feelings of deep enjoyment. All problems seem to disappear, and the world circles without being noticed; there is an exhilarating sense of transcendence.

Children naturally experience this intense, contentedly concentrated state. I always felt it was my role as parent or supervisor to help children discover the activities that brought them happiness. "Never bother a happy child" is a rule repeated frequently to my grown children, now with families of their own. Let a child eat dinner after everyone else. The bath can go to tomorrow. The child has entered a happy state of concentrated attention. You want this to become a habit. Don't rob the child of the opportunity to practice *eutrapelia*.

J. Robert Oppenheimer, the nuclear physicist, reported, "There are children playing in the street who could solve some of my top problems in physics, because they have modes of sensory perception that I lost long ago." Indeed, as a child Albert Einstein asked himself a naive question he lacked the mathematical skills to answer: What would the world look like if he could sit astride a speeding beam of light, and what would that speeding beam of light look like if he could also travel racing beside it? Other great scientific minds were seeking to dislodge the secrets of the universe, but they were so limited by their adult preconceptions, that they failed to ask the right questions. In 1905 when Einstein was twenty-six, he had finally developed the intellectual capacity to answer the question that began with his childlike sense of playful wonder. *The Special Theory of Relativity* was published and would radically change the way the world considered itself in relationship to space, time and light.

Another story, e-mailed to me recently, illustrates the childlike tendency to find the obvious in the sublime:

"If I sold my house and my car," asked the Sunday school

teacher, "and had a big garage sale and gave all my money to the church, would that get me into heaven?"

"NO!" the children all answered.

"If I cleaned the church every day, mowed the yard, and kept everything neat and tidy, would that get me into heaven?"

Again, the answer was, "NO!"

"Well, then, if I was kind to animals and gave candy to all the children and loved my wife, would that get me into heaven?"

Again, they all answered, "NO!"

"Then how can I get into Heaven?"

A five-year-old boy shouted out, "YOU GOTTA BE DEAD!"

In truth, you gotta be dead to get to heaven, dead to the old self-life, the sophisticated sense of arrogant intellectualism that stews in the poison of its own pride. Playfulness, laughter and *eutrapelia* can lead us to answers that hide beneath the surface of things and deliver us from the fixations on ourselves from which so many suffer.

WONDER

Another childlike quality that makes us fit to receive the kingdom of God is an innocent credulity, the kind of easy belief that allows for discovery. "A child's world is fresh and new and beautiful, full of wonder and excitement. It is our misfortune that for most of us that clear-eyed vision, that true instinct for what is beautiful and awe-inspiring, is dimmed and even lost before we reach adulthood," wrote Rachel Carson, the bestselling nature writer, in her book *A Sense of Wonder*.

Carson recommends that if a child is to keep this inborn sense of wonder, he needs the companionship of at least one adult who can share it, rediscovering with him the mystery of the world. "Rediscovering" is the pivotal word. Perhaps we adults need the child's company as much as the child needs ours. Carson's additional assessment rings true: "I sincerely believe that for the child, for the parent seeking to guide him, it is not half so important to know as to feel. If facts are the seeds that later produce knowledge and wisdom, then the emotions and the impressions of the senses are the fertile soil in which the seeds must grow."

Wonder and an ability to believe often go hand in hand. We stand in awe of something that captures our attention; curiosity begins to rise as to why or how this phenomenon comes to be; curiosity leads to research, then we stand humbled by the magnitude of what we are discovering. "Isn't it wonderful?" we say in the learning. "Isn't this fascinating? How beautiful!"

Sir Francis Bacon, almost four hundred years ago, wrote that wonder—which he felt was the seed of knowledge—was the reflection of the purest form of pleasure. It is that kind of pleasure we must recapture if we are to take joy in the world as an expression of the personality of God. This kind of delight opens us to learning, to discovery, to the ability to believe in what is spiritually true. We will begin to stand amazed at the incarnation that is still redeeming us in every way, as the little girl does in John Shea's poem "Sharon's Christmas Prayer."

She was five,
sure of the facts,
and recited them
with slow solemnity
convinced every word
was revelation.

She said
they were so poor
they had only peanut butter and jelly sandwiches
to eat.
and they went a long way from home
without getting lost. The lady rode
a donkey, the man walked, and the baby
was inside the lady.
They had to stay in a stable
with an ox and an ass (tee-hee)
but the Three Rich Men found them
because a star lited the roof

Shepherds came and you could
pet the sheep but not feed them.
Then the baby was borned.
And do you know who he was?
Her quarter eyes inflated
to silver dollars.
The baby was God.

And she jumped in the air
whirled around, dove into the sofa
and buried her head under the cushion
which is the only proper response
to the Good News of the Incarnation.

John Shea

Most of us, some highly trained in theological truths, have lost
the childlike ability to find God in the commonplace; we can only
find him as we have created him to be in the rationalized terrain
of our own minds. We experience the incarnation as historical
fact, not as ongoing experiential revelation. We no longer "jump
in the air, whirl around, dive into the sofa, or bury our heads un-

der the cushion"—a most proper response to evident divine intervention.

This idea was affirmed in *The Most Reluctant Convert,* David Downing's biography of the conversion of C. S. Lewis. For Lewis, the author writes:

> Boyhood had been a kind of "fall" from childhood. For him becoming a "grown-up" would be a further step in the wrong direction. Through his autobiography, as well as in Lewis's fiction, *grown-up* usually connotes a state of dreary practicality, in which utility and "getting ahead" predominate, or where the sneerings of boyhood take on even more sinister manifestations. For him, the path less taken involved a return to a childhood sense of wonder and glory instead of submitting to the mundanities and inanities he found all too prevalent in modern life.

We must work to restore that childlike wonder that allows us to discover God in what is at hand, what is nearby, with what is in the everyday world that surrounds our everyday lives. The Catholic scholar Ronald Rolheiser writes in *The Holy Longing* that God is all around us.

> God takes on flesh so that every home becomes a church, every child becomes the Christ-child, and all food and drink become a sacrament. God's many faces are now everywhere, in flesh, tempered and turned down, so that our human eyes can see him. God, in his many-faced face, has become as accessible, and visible, as the nearest water tap.

The God Hunt is one of the correctives for our lost wonder and delight. It is the way we cry out to God, "Did you see me do that? Were you watching?" It is also (wonderfully) the way he cries out to us, "Did you catch that? Were you looking? You can't believe what I'm going to do next! Attend!"

I hired a fly-by-night handyman to repair the broken plasterboard in the attic floor of the garage. He was cheap, smelled of alcohol, and the work got done. I was grateful to have the unsightly holes finally repaired and asked him to look at the wood framing around the upstairs windows, which was also in bad shape.

"Lady," he said, "you've got so much water damage, the glass is about to fall through!" Then he nailed some boards in place to keep the glass from falling and suggested I call my insurance company. I never saw him again, but I called the insurance company and they said they'd replace the windows. God does use strange messengers from time to time!

SEEKING AND FINDING

Before we begin, let us also be aware of the paradoxical nature of the God Hunt. God is not only the One who hides, but he is also the One who seeks. We cannot find him unless he calls us to the chase. Theologically, this quality refers to the fact that God is prevenient. Everything originates in him, and he is before all things. Men and women can do nothing unless God first gives them the desire. So he calls, "Come and find me! I will be found by you." Jeremiah 29:13 is an invitation to the sacred hide-and-seek, "You will seek me and find me when you seek me with all your heart."

Let us pray that we will be given the desire to seek him. Abraham Kuyper, Dutch theologian and politician (he served a term as Holland's prime minister), in his classic devotional *To Be Near unto God,* writes 110 meditations on a single thought from Psalm 73: "As for me, it is good to be near unto God." He compares the heart of the true believer to the heart of the nominally religious person, who cries out to God only when he is in need.

> With the devout believer in God, it is altogether different. He seeks his Father. He knows by experience that it is possible, even here on earth, to hold fellowship with that Father Who is in heaven. He has knowledge of "the secret walk with God." From blessed experience he knows that in this secret walk, fellowship is mutual, so then not only he seeks his Father, but the Father also lets Himself be found of His child.

We hunt for him. He hides. He seeks us while we look for him. He finds us. We find him. This is a theological complementary contradiction and we can scarcely understand it. We can scarcely comprehend that God delights in us. "We were made not primarily that we should love God (though we were made for that too) but that God may love us, that we may become objects in which the Divine love may be 'well pleased,' " writes C. S. Lewis about achieving happiness. The God who delights in us is the kind of God who takes joy in the fact that we have set our faces to the finding of him.

When our children were small, we taught them to hunt for God in the world. It was remarkable how easily they could identify answered prayers, evidence of God's care and his help to be agents of kindness in the world. When they sighted God, they called out, "I spy! I spy God!" As they grew older, they used more sophisticated terminology such as, "Today I had a God Hunt sighting." This language of holy hunting, no matter their ages, was accessible and demythologized the weighty verbal theology that often chokes up everyday communications. It is easier for children and parents to talk spontaneously about I spys than to discuss the weighty fact that God is omnipresent, omniscient or omnipotent.

When our youngest son, Jeremy, was eleven years old, we prayed at the beginning of the school year that he would make good friends. Highly motivated and very creative, Jeremy designed a game that soon occupied eleven of his classmates who traipsed in and out of the house over a period of months. One day he came home to announce, "I had three 'I spys' today." Jeremy had friends in abundance, and many of his "I spys" related to our answered prayer.

So let us play the game the way we did when we were children, and let us play it like children do, with our whole hearts, as hardy play. Deuteronomy 4:29 instructs the people of Israel, "But if from there you seek the LORD your God, you will find him if you look for him with all your heart and with all your soul."

THE RED THREAD

Before we go on, however, we must understand the difference between beginning the God Hunt with *childlikeness* and beginning it with *childishness,* which is an indicator of immaturity. Let me illustrate this from the life of a great writer, Hans Christian Andersen. Born in abject poverty in 1782, Andersen was keenly ashamed of his humble beginnings. Awkward, unsociable and haunted by a family history of insanity, the young boy seemed an unlikely candidate for greatness.

Yet, critics now assess that his contribution to literature through the fairy tale was immense. While a few authors before him had collected tales from oral tradition, Andersen was the first to treat the peasant lore as genuine literature and to invent new tales which had the power to enter into the collective consciousness. Just mention "The Ugly Duckling," for instance, and even those who do not know the name of its author have a concept of the tale as story, but even more, as a powerful mythic truth.

Thus, childlikeness in Andersen worked good for him. The wonder and delight allowed him to view the world in remarkably original fashion and to create a genre that transformed the works of all those who came after him. Andersen's biographer Jackie Wullschlager writes:

> The benefits Andersen brought to English children's literature were inestimable. He gave the fairy tale a key place in nineteenth-century culture. He showed that writing for children and literary and imaginative talent could go together. He introduced the idea of fantasy in children's stories, preparing the climate for Lewis Carroll in the 1860s. And in creating a separate children's world of talking toys and animals, he had a profound effect on later classics of childhood such as *The Wind in the Willows* and *Winnie the Pooh*. This legacy continues in contemporary Anglo-Saxon children's culture, from Disney remakes of fairy tales to films such as *Toy Story*.

Yet, childishness worked ill in him. Though Hans Christian overcame his past, his unquenchable desire for significance—a remnant of his impoverished childhood—controlled his manhood. A driven narcissistic artist, he was the classic neurotic. All his tales were about himself in one way or another; Andersen was a compulsive autobiographer—in his letters, in his diaries and in his writing. He is the morbidly sensitive princess who cannot stand a pea through twenty stacked mattresses. He is the ugly duckling, the little match girl and the tin soldier.

Much to the dismay of people who knew him well, Andersen never grew up. The genius who created the little child in "The Emperor's New Clothes" and destroyed the sham of the aristocratic adult society could also be annoying in his childishness. Wullschlager quotes one witness who described Hans Christian Andersen as "a child, according to the ideal of childhood; keenly sensitive, entirely egotistical, innocently vain, the centre of life, interest, concern and meaning to himself, perfectly unconscious that there existed another standard, an outer circle, taking it for granted that everywhere he was to be first and all. . . . He had no notion of time, and as pertinaciously required everyone to be at his beck and call as any curled darling in the nursery who is at once the plague and the joy of his household."

Yet even a tormented genius like Hans Christian Andersen understood that God is all around us, and he found moments of peace in choosing to see God's intervention. Speaking before a crowd of working men, he made an astute assessment of his own work:

> In England, in the royal navy, through all the rigging, small and great ropes, there runs a red thread, signifying that it belongs to the crown; through all men's lives there runs also a thread, invisible indeed, that shows we belong to God. To find this thread in small and great, in our own life and in all about us, the poet's art helps us.

Working out of his better self, putting aside the petty vanities that often consumed him, Andersen was from time to time able to find the red thread. May we too find the red thread, invisible indeed, that runs through all the rigging, through the small and great ropes. Let us begin the hunt, capturing the best of childlikeness, seeking for God as he penetrates our world.

Sighting

Liz McFadzean, from La Canada, California, is a practiced God hunter. She dipped into an ordinary day to find this divine intervention:

Today is my tennis day. I play every Friday with a couple of friends. On Tuesday I saw my doctor about a little tendonitis in my right thumb. She asked me not to play tennis for a week in order to let it rest. Not to be waylaid in my plans, I whined and said, "But I want to play." My doctor relented but strongly recommended that I put ice on it after my game.

Last night one of my tennis pals cancelled because of a conflict. The other called this morning with a stuffy nose. My Friday game is off! Do you think God did that for me to take care of me when I wouldn't take care of myself? I am thanking him today, because my God cares more about my welfare than I do. What a great, kind loving God we have.

3

Going the Wrong Way
to Buffalo

*The cry to God as Father in the New Testament is not a calm
acknowledgement of a universal truth about God's abstract "fatherhood,"
it is the child's cry out of nightmare.*

ROWAN WILLIAMS

I drove the wrong way to Buffalo. My husband and I had been
visiting close friends in the mountains beside the Appalachian
Trail above Charlottesville, Virginia. We were on our way to the
Shakespeare Festival in Stratford, Ontario, with a stop at the airport in Buffalo, New York, to pick up a couple from New Orleans
who were accompanying us to our much anticipated theatre ex-
travaganza—five plays in three days. Obviously we needed to
leave early in order to meet their flight on time, cross the border,
drive west across Canada, check into the bed and breakfast and be
ready for the performance that evening.

"I'll drive," I volunteered, being most alert in the morning. Before we joined the freeway (Route 81 going north toward Buffalo),
we stopped for gas and a newspaper. I turned onto the highway, my
mind troubled by our recent visit—my dear friend was fighting
what was to become a losing battle with cancer—and David settled
down in the passenger's seat, totally absorbed in his reading.

After about half an hour it suddenly hit me: the road signs were all showing that the mileage to Roanoke was decreasing. *Roanoke! I don't want to go to Roanoke. I want to go to Buffalo.* "David," I said, dreading his reaction. "I hate to say this, but I think I've been driving in the wrong direction. That last sign said I'm going toward Roanoke, Virginia."

His head popped up from behind the papers and he twisted around as though he could read through the marker we had just passed. "Roanoke! That's south! We don't want to go south. We want to go to north. You're supposed to be driving to Buffalo!"

Now I knew this. He didn't have to tell me. Neither did he have to remind me of the arrival time of our friends at the airport. Determined to do it right, I pulled off at the next exit, turned around and proceeded to drive the right way to Buffalo. By pushing the pedal, navigating Route 81 in the correct direction, we made it to the airport just a few minutes before the Louisiana flight landed.

Needless to say, if you go one-half hour the wrong way, even with the right intentions, you still have to go back one-half hour pointed in the correct direction until you get where you started. That's a total of one hour lost in a tight morning of driving!

Literature is filled with stories of people going in the wrong direction. C. S. Lewis tells of arriving as a young student to study at Oxford and not being able to find the campus. Trudging from the train station with his baggage, he kept looking for the "fabled cluster of spires and towers" so many had mentioned before him. After walking awhile, dismayed by the shabbiness of some of the houses he was passing, he realized he was heading for open country, and it was only when he turned and looked back that he could see the majestic towers. They were on the opposite side of town from where he had stopped. He had been going in the wrong direction. In *The Great Divorce* Lewis writes,

I do not think that all who choose wrong roads perish; but their rescue consists in being put back on the right road. A wrong sum can be put right: but only by going back till you find the error and working it afresh from that point, never by simply going on. Evil can be undone, but it cannot "develop" into good. Time does not heal it.

Ian McEwan's novel *Atonement* looks closely at the difficulty of going the right way once a wrong turn has been taken. It is the story of thirteen-year-old Briony Tallis, a youngster whose narcissism demands that she be the center of everyone's concern. On the hottest day of the summer of 1934, she watches, hidden from her bedroom window, as her older sister, Celia, strips off her clothes and plunges into the courtyard fountain of the family's country estate. Standing amazed by the pool is Robbie Turner, a childhood friend who has just come home from Cambridge.

From this incident the over-imaginative and over-wrought adolescent contrives a fabrication that will eventually destroy the lives of many around her. Later that evening Briony accuses Robbie of raping a cousin. Accusations are made; legalities swoop in with inexorable finality; Robbie will go to jail; the sisters will be forever divided; family and friendships will be shattered; and Briony is forced to hold to this lie even when years later the true identity of the violator is revealed. She spends the rest of her life attempting to make amends for the consequences of a lie that she can never change.

These examples illustrate that in order to get where we want to go, we must point ourselves in the right direction. Theologians call this repentance, this turning around and going in the right direction. Mostly it is initiated by sorrow over past doings. Let's look instead at a different example of going in the right direction—one that is driven by love.

GOD'S PASSION

Think for a moment about a man and a woman who can't bear the thought of separation, who make as many contacts during the day as possible, and whose minds are continually wandering back to dear and cherished thoughts about the loved one. They think about each other first thing in the morning; they may dream about each other during the night. The hour is never too late to make a phone call to end the day.

This passion, viewed as silly or embarrassing by the outsider (who may have experienced something similar long ago, or who was disappointed in love, or who has watched romance fade beneath the weightiness and responsibilities of marriage), is more divine than any of us really understand. Oh, yes, you say. You are going to tell me that I should have this kind of passion for God.

Well, that may be partly true, but what I really want to say is that God has this kind of passion for you. You see, God can't get you off his mind. That first surging thrill when two people realize the attraction each feels is mutual, that infatuation a parent feels for his newborn—this never fades for God. He never slips into the neglectful weightiness of floundering marriage. He is not guilty of infidelity or of neglect. He doesn't keep looking for someone else better. You are his beloved. Further, this Lover of my Soul, though the Ancient of Days, is always young, athletic and eager for me. "Listen! My lover! Look! Here he comes, leaping across the mountains, bounding over the hills. My lover is like a gazelle or a young stag. Look! There he stands behind our wall, gazing through the windows, peering through the lattice" (Song of Songs 2:8-9).

Alan Jones writes, "Christianity is a love affair beginning with the gasp of astonishment with which all love affairs begin." Indeed, God has fallen in love with you and can't wait until you turn your full attention his way. Unfortunately, most of us do not regularly reciprocate God's passion. Instead, we behave like the spouse who dutifully makes love (has to be coaxed into it, actually), then rolls over in bed with a sigh that the exercise is finally over and falls asleep. We act like the neglectful husband who only thinks of work first thing in the morning. We are unfaithful, making clandestine appointments with someone other than our true love.

Most of us have no idea how far away we have been traveling from the heart of God or for how long. The signposts are all telling us we are journeying in the wrong direction. Preoccupied with our own affairs, we just haven't been paying attention.

Our neglect and unfaithfulness grieves our Lover. Indeed, many Scripture passages record God weeping over a defiled betrothal covenant, a discarded engagement ring in his hand. "Where are you?" he cries throughout history again and again. Look at his reaction to the tragic betrayals in so many Old Testament passages. We see his actions as pronounced judgments on the two-timing Israelites who sneakily cuckolded the Divine Lover, but they are really the wail of a broken-hearted, jilted lover. Even knowing how Judah and Israel deserve all the awful events that occur in their national history because they have gone whoring, God's soul waxes between longing and rage. Hosea 11:8-9, set within the context of a prophet married to a whore, captures the painful ambiguity:

> How can I give you up, Ephraim?
>> How can I hand you over, Israel?
> How can I treat you like Admah?
>> How can I make you like Zeboiim?
> My heart is changed within me;
>> all my compassion is aroused.

I will not carry out my fierce anger,
      nor will I turn and devastate Ephraim;
For I am God and not man—
      the Holy One among you.
      I will not come in wrath.

With regularity we all need to ask, How far have I wandered from this startling passion? Who has abandoned whom? When it comes to infidelity, who has created the triangle? Who is it I really desire? Whose touch do I long for at the end of the day or whose embrace when circumstances are difficult? Whose breath do I wish for at the back of my neck when I am resting? Who do I think of first thing when I wake? Whom do I call on the minute, on the hour? How much joy swells my being when I hear the sound of the Lover's voice? Do I make a point of disciplining myself to seek him whenever my mind has a moment of repose? Better yet, is he always, always, at the back of my consciousness?

No? Look at the map of your soul. You didn't know it, but you have traveled far from where you should be. A slight mistake in navigation, a detour despite the warnings, can cause an irreparable error in destination. We want to be heading home toward him, going his way, running along beside him, catching up and getting in step, grabbing his hand, holding onto his elbow. He is the loved one and the loving one. He woos, pursues, seeks you out in a crowd, whispers your name with tenderness, over and over, and waits, endlessly it seems, for you to join with him in the delightful activity of seeking and finding.

RESTORING OUR SPIRITUAL PASSION

Orthopraxy, right living, is as important as and a complement to orthodoxy, right doctrine. How we act is a validation of what we believe, and what we truly believe informs everything we think, do or say. Are you in love with the One who loves you passionately? Do your actions reveal that you believe he loves you and that you return his ardor? Did you practice anything in this day that was proof that you really believe God is love and that he is crazy in love with you?

Are you rushing forth into the days anticipating eagerly the ways you are going to meet, to playfully cry, "Gotcha!"? Or was two weeks ago, or two months ago (whenever you were last in church), the last time you had a concentrated focus on things spiritual, before you stepped outside, and the sermon-sucking black hole that exists somewhere between the front door and the parking lot swooshed all remembrance of worship into its vortex? Truthfully you haven't looked into the Word since, and you really haven't thought much about God.

The Barna Research Group has been tracking America's religious beliefs and practices since 1984 and over that time has given us an alarming picture of the state of the church. Of those who meet the requirements for being classified as born-again, the data confirms that there are more than ten million who are unchurched. Now, we can love God without going to church, but we can't love him as well. The community of faith is one of the primary places where we have the best opportunities to work out the orthopraxy of our orthodoxy.

What begins to be even more disturbing is when The Barna Group measures nine religious beliefs that have also been tracked for the past decade. These include the self-reported importance of faith, levels of personal commitment to Christianity and to Jesus Christ, beliefs about God, Satan and the Bible, and perspectives on eternal salvation. These beliefs dip into some core values of orthodox doctrine and many are disquietingly diluted.

For instance, one of the most disturbing revelations concerns the nature of Christ. Described in Barna's book *State of the Church 2002* is the large number of born-again, non-evangelicals (measured according to established criteria) who believe that Jesus sinned. One out of five strongly agree that he sinned, an additional one out of eight agreed less vehemently, and 6 percent disagreed somewhat, with 5 percent not sure what to believe. This means that nearly half of the non-evangelical born-again segment, 46 percent, did not strongly disagree with the notion that Christ sinned.

Barna's concludes:

America certainly did not experience the spiritual revival that many Christians hoped would emerge as the new millennium began. In fact, Americans seem to have become almost inoculated to spiritual events, outreach efforts and the quest for personal spiritual development. There are magnificent exceptions through the country, but overall, Christian ministry is stuck in a deep rut. Our research continues to point out the need for behavioral modeling, strategic ministry and a more urgent reliance upon God to change people's lives. Like the churches of Laodicea and Sardis, described in the Bible as distasteful to God because of their complacency and spiritual deadness, too many Christians and churches in America have traded in spiritual passion for empty rituals, clever methods and mindless practices. The challenge to today's Church is not methodological. It is a challenge to resuscitate the spiritual passion and fervor of the nation's Christians.

How are you going to resuscitate or energize your spiritual passion? Going on the God Hunt can restore practical Christianity and help you renew and freshen the reality of the Lover who is always there, waiting to laughingly play. As quickly as any of the spiritual practices that have been traditionally undertaken by Christians through the centuries, the God Hunt can restore delight and wonder again to our understanding of a life of faith. It is a much-needed exercise for Christians who seem to be mired in spiritual complacency. It is daily evidence of how much God loves to be with us and of how constantly we are on his mind.

A SMALL DEVIATION

Brunelleschi's Dome, by Ross King, is a fascinating account of one of the great structural engineering feats of the Renaissance. In 1418 Filippo Brunelleschi, a goldsmith and clockmaker, not a master builder, undertook the huge task (twenty-eight years worth of work) of solving how to raise a dome over Florence's new cathedral, Santa Maria del Fiore. The story of how Brunelleschi contrived to move an estimated seventy million pounds of brick, stone and wood scaffolding some hundreds of feet into the air is the story of a genius reinventing the architecture of his time.

During the construction of the dome, in 1420, a manuscript was discovered that told the story of an aqueduct that was built through the mountains above the town of Saldae, Algeria, in A.D. 148. Nonius Datus, a Roman hydraulic engineer, was sent to survey the terrain, draw up cross sections of the mountain, calculate the axis of the tunnel, then oversee the teams of excavators who began digging opposite each other at different sides. Four years later Nonius was frantically called back. The teams had each committed minor deviations and were not going to meet in the middle as planned. Managing to rectify the errors, Nonius observed that if he had arrived a little later, there would have been two tunnels in the mountain!

At the time, the discovery of this old record must have caused
concern to the eight teams of masons, each constructing a sepa-
rate wall of the octagonal dome. Since they too were laying brick
and mortar on opposite sides, how could they insure that their
work would converge at the top?

"One of the keys to raising the dome," writes King, "was the
precise calculation and measurement of each horizontal layer of
brick or stone as it was added in a gradually contracting sequence.
But how would these measurements be taken? How could the
curvature of the eight individual walls be controlled during the
process of construction? The difficulty was made even more acute
by the fact that each wall had to incorporate two shells rising in
tandem, as well as their supporting ribs. A deviation of only several inches in one of these ribs—each of which was over one hundred feet in length—meant that the connection, like that at
Saldae, would not be achieved." No one, even today, is quite sure
how Brunelleschi succeeded, but the dome has stood in place now
for over five hundred years and is still the highest in the world at
143 feet in diameter.

The Christian life could be compared to the building of
Brunelleschi's dome or the tunnel at Sardae. A small deviation,
taken at some point in the direction of our lives, can result in a
yawning cataclysm later on. We become secular Christians without knowing it. Our loyalties are divided, but we will argue hotly
if challenged. Christ pegged us well, "These people honor me
with their lips, but their hearts are far from me. They worship me
in vain; their teachings are but rules taught by men" (Matthew
15:8-9). We are Christians in name, living out a kind of theological schizophrenia.

Sometimes we do not develop the long-term intimacy that allows us to recognize God's daily intervention in our lives because

we are moving away from familiarity, traveling along a trajectory that is hastening us far from the heart of the Father. At other times we have chosen to act in a way that closes us up in a room without a door. Now, all the work of our hands cannot atone for what has been done. It is not in our power to make things right. The divine chase has been abandoned. We are not seeking, only running away.

A plaque hung in my hallway reminds me, *Vocatus atque non vocatus, Deus aderit.* "Bidden or unbidden, God is present." His nature is not dependent on my acknowledgment of it. His imminence and transcendence do not exist only when I recognize these qualities. I may be going in the wrong direction, but his is always the right way. I may have destroyed my own future, but God is always the perfect past, present and future. He still desires to restore childlikeness to my battered, aged soul. "Let's play," he calls. "Where are you?"

SOMEBODY IS WATCHING

I have seen M. Night Shyamalan's film *Signs,* starring Mel Gibson, twice. The first time I came away thinking, *Hmmm, that was interesting.* I am not much taken with alien invasion plots, but I did recognize that the story is only ostensibly science-fiction; it is really a story of a man who has turned his back on God and, in wounded rebellion, is going the wrong way. Then a pastor pointed out to me how many evidences there were of God intervening to bring the hero of the film back to faith. The second time I sat in the darkened movie theater with my son Joel, who has a degree in film and scriptwriting. I made notes on a legal pad and tried to keep my thumb on the line so I wouldn't overwrite and be unable to read what I had written in the light.

The film is about an Episcopalian priest, Graham Hess, whose wife dies after being hit by a car when the driver nods to sleep at the wheel. This tragic incident has bereft the husband of love, orphaned his two small children and precipitated the father into a state of unbelief. He has torn off the clerical collar and resigned his pastoral position in the church of a small town somewhere in Bucks County, Pennsylvania. Hess tells townspeople to no longer address him as Father. In one intense scene, he refuses to pray the blessing over the meal. "No more prayers. There will be no more energy or time wasted over prayers in this family."

The lives of this family are not what they had been. The young son has taken on the responsibility of mothering his little sister, Bo, who manifests symptomatic signs of distress. She can't drink a whole glass of water. "It's contaminated," she explains with her baby lisp. "It's dirty. It has a hair in it." Half-filled glasses of water get left on counters, on the television and on tables. Merrill, Graham's single brother, is a has-been baseball player who never made it to the major leagues (he held the record for the longest home-run ever hit in the minors—but also for the most strike outs). He has moved back to the family farm, taking up residence in the room above the garage to help during this time of bereavement and sorrowful adjustment.

Mysterious crop-signs have suddenly appeared in the cornfields of the farm. Is this the work of unfeeling pranksters, or are the signs directional signals for alien visitors? The German Shepherds display anxiety, barking, growling and even turning against the Hess children. What is going on? Finally the national news reports that crop-signs are appearing all over the world, and unaccounted hovering lights have been seen over Mexico City.

At this point a profound conversation takes place between Graham and Merrill, who wants to be comforted. "There are two kinds of people," says the former minister. "When something lucky happens, there are those who see it as evidence that there is Someone out there looking out for them. They see signs. They see evidences. The other kind of people feel that whatever happens, they are on their own. Luck is just coincidence." Throughout the plot, that line is repeated, "It's just coincidence. It's just coincidence."

The "signs" of the film's title are about spiritual evidences; the aliens and the potential hostile invasion are used as a plot device, a metaphor for those unaccountable and uncontrollable terrors that assault us. Do they point to a God who is looking out for us, or are they just coincidences and we are really alone in the world? As it turns out, pranksters are not making the crop-signs. The circles in the fields are doom's reality—directional signs to guide an alien invasion with hostile intentions to harvest the bodies of humans for some unidentified purpose.

The Hess family spends a night of terror in their boarded up farmhouse. When the attic is breached by an advance alien contingent, the four retreat to the basement. This trauma sets off a severe asthma attack in Graham's son, Morgan. In a powerful scene, Graham holds his son, the child's lungs swelling as he struggles for breath and life. "Breathe with me," the father says. In and out, in and out, they labor for breath together. "Don't be afraid, Morgan. Breathe with me. You and I are the same. Together; breathe with me."

We hear the prayer of Graham to the God he no longer believes exists, *Don't do this to me. Don't do this to me. I hate you. I hate you.* Yet the visual juxtaposition is profound, the terrified human father is holding the suffering son in a pietà-form that shows how the heavenly Father God holds us in moments of deepest terror, when we are gasping for air. He whispers the same message, *Breathe with me. Don't be afraid. You and I are the same. Breathe with me.*

Throughout this terrible night, as the family is holed up in the cellar, listening to boarded doors rattling, footsteps padding upstairs, the baby monitor picking up signals and the sounds of household items crashing, we see flashbacks of the terrible accident that had all but severed the body of Graham's wife in two. In the flashbacks she is holding onto life, still talking because she has something she feels compelled to say. "It was meant to be," she says to Graham, as he struggles for control beside her. The pieces of emerging memory give us the full final message. *Tell Graham to see. See. Tell Merrill to keep swinging.*

The morning comes. All is quiet upstairs. The boy rests peacefully, having survived the night, but he is not strong enough to endure another asthma attack. The men risk leaving their sanctuary to get his medicine. Upstairs, news reports announce that due to some ancient ritual enacted by the people of the Middle East, the hovering alien warships have departed. All is clear. Graham places his weakened son on the living room sofa, goes to move the television set from the cubby beneath the stairs where they had huddled listening to news accounts, and to his horror he sees that the alien who has been laying siege to their house has not departed. He is holding the unconscious body of Morgan, who is limp again in asthmatic arrest. The alien emits a poisonous vapor into the child's nostrils.

The last words spoken by Graham's wife suddenly give clarity. "Swing away," he calls to Merrill. "Swing away!" The former baseball player grabs the record-setting home run bat mounted in a place of honor on the living room wall and begins whomping the alien. Graham grabs the lifeless body of his son and rushes to the yard. The medicine he has already retrieved is in his hand; he stabs the hypodermic needle into the flesh and pushes the plunger. Inside, Merrill gives the alien another whack, shoving the hostile intruder into furniture where one of the dozens of half-drunk glasses of water falls on him, then another. This is the ancient ritual, a water baptism that protects against the intruders that bring terror. Another whack, more glasses spill their contents, overcoming the enemy.

Merrill rushes to the lawn where the child is still comatose. Suddenly Morgan stirs; he lives. "Did someone save me?" the boy asks. Graham realizes that because of the asthma attack, his son's lungs were closed. No poison has reached them. He holds his child to his heart and whispers, "I think Someone did."

Then the prophetic words open his soul with greatest clarity, "Tell Graham to see. Tell Graham to see." See the

David was conducting a training conference for pastors in Michigan. After he had finished and everyone had gone, he went to pack the teaching materials back into our car and discovered he had a flat tire. At that moment a man drove into the church parking lot. "Do you know where I could get this fixed?" my husband inquired.

"Sure," said the man and directed David to a tire place a block away, where they removed a nail, patched the tire and inflated it—all for fifteen dollars. Without that direction David would have had no idea where to go.

signs all around. See the son's life-threatening condition as given by God to protect him from ill intents. See the water-fixation of his daughter as a means by which God has provided a way to combat the threatening terror. See the home run record baseball bat as a weapon to defend against the enemy.

"There are no coincidences," the clergyman concludes. "There are no coincidences." This is the powerful point of the whole film. Nothing occurs without design. There is Somebody watching out for us even when we choose to go the wrong way. The signs of this are all around.

LIFE MAZES

This summer David and I spoke at Camp Meeting in the Lancaster, Pennsylvania, area. Since we were driving from Chicago, we decided to take our nine-year-old granddaughter with us, and Caitlyn and I explored the Amish countryside. One delightful morning was spent at the Cherry-Crest Farm Amazing Maize Maze, five acres of corn over your head that take an estimated hour to work your way through, if you don't get lost.

At age nine, Caitlyn much preferred petting all the animals in the farm zoo and holding the newly hatched chicks, so that was the way we spent a delightful morning. At one point we stood on a bridge high above the corn maze where we could look down on families and groups starting to work together to uncover the clues that would lead them through the maze to the exit. Each team was given a flag to wave high if they needed help so that the Maze Master sitting on a lifeguard-like tower could steer them through the paths.

I kept thinking about how frequently when we are wandering through life mazes, we take the wrong turns, get lost, forget to read the clues, sit down in a pout, get angry, get tired, howl so constantly we can't hear anyone answer, conclude no one is there to help us, tear up the rules, throw down our emergency flag, stomp on it, sit down in frustration, wail and whine, go into a panic attack, hyperventilate, then turn to despair. A devious voice on our left shoulder insinuates, *You're never going to get out of here, you know. No one cares about coming to find you, got it? Nothing is going to change. This will never end. What did you think you were doing, taking on a life maze after all? Plenty of people are still lost in here. Never going to hear about them again.*

Wait. Wait. Shut up. Whether you know it or not, choose to see it or not, believe it or not, there is a Maze Master who can guide us out of wrong turns, silence ventilation sessions, calm our child-like rebellions and get us safely home before night, which is coming on fast. He's just a little above the eye-line, but he has not left the field because we are lost. It all depends upon how we choose to read the emergency signs.

SAUL AND DAVID

Saul and David were two kingly characters in the Old Testament who each reacted to evidences of God's work in opposite ways. The older king, Saul, had become obsessed with the idea that David, a young warrior, was a rival to his throne. Indeed, because of Saul's own disobedience, God had rejected him and had instructed the prophet Samuel to choose another king after God's heart. David was that chosen man, and since the day of his anointing the youth had risen to become the favored redeemer of a nation, a warrior loved by men and women alike.

A royal hunt to ensure dynastic succession ensues with Saul hounding David over the land. The book of 1 Samuel tells of two incidents where God delivered the king into the hands of his rival, but David refused to harm "God's anointed" (chapters 24 and 26). The first episode occurred in the Desert of En Gedi when Saul slipped into a cave to relieve himself. In the dark, that close, David slices off a piece of his skirt with his sword. "My lord the king!" he cries, standing outside after Saul has left. He holds up the severed cloth as a sign that God had delivered royalty into the hands of the fugitive and that David had chosen not to butcher him. Saul understands and promises safety, but the pledge is not to be kept.

Again, in the wilderness of Ziph, Saul comes against David's band of refugees with three thousand of Israel's best fighting men. David and Abishai, one of his elect commanders, creep into the encampment by night, abscond the spear from where it has been struck into the ground, and the water jug by the sleeping king's side. In a loud voice, standing atop a mountain, David chides Saul's commander Abner and his army for not having guarded the king. He waves his proofs before them. Then he calls out to Saul, "Why is my lord pursuing his servant? What have I done, and what wrong am I guilty of?" (1 Samuel 26:18). Saul repents, but it is not a turning in another direction that lasts, so David escapes to the land of the Philistines (27:1).

When faced with the same evidence—God anointing David as king—these two men chose to respond in different fashions. David sees God's hand and at the peril of his own life and despite the insistence of his companions, he refuses to use it as an excuse for regicide. Saul repents, but allows consuming jealousy and a pattern of instability to overrule. He sees the signs that God has delivered him into the hands of his rival and understands that he has been spared. Saul speaks the truth aloud, repents of his pursuit, but cannot keep from the obsessive need to obliterate the young warrior (dangerous to his future kingdom); indeed, David is his own son-in-law, and the closest friend to his beloved heir, Jonathan.

Even reading the signs correctly, we can go in the wrong direction, if we so choose. Saul's choices lead him and his sons into peril and eventual destruction. David's choices receive God's approval, and the maze of his life, his years of wandering and hiding in the wilderness, eventually lead him to the throne and rulership.

OLLIE OLLIE OXEN FREE

I recently decided to research the etymology of the phrase "ollie ollie oxen free," the signal given at the end of hide-and-seek that the hunt is over or the main player has given up hope of winning. The Internet site World Wide Words explains the meaning behind the words: "One guess is that the original was something like 'all in free' for 'all who are out can come in free,' to indicate that the person who is 'it' in the game of hide-and-seek has caught somebody to become the new 'it,' so everybody else can come out of hiding without the risk of being caught." Supposedly oral transmission has garbled the words, with "all in" becoming "ollie" and "outs in free" becoming "oxen free."

Are you far from home base? Listen, listen: perhaps you are not nearly as far away as you think. "It" is shouting the signal, "All in free! All in free!" Yes, you may have to run for a while. You may be a bit breathless and frantic when you return to the game. You will have to promise not to cheat again, not to wander so far. You will have to apologize for causing such concern (and you will have to mean it). But look! There is time. There is still a lingering glow in the western sky. The fireflies are beginning to blink. The evening air is warm and inviting, and the game will not be called for the night until you are returned safely to the waiting arms of your laughing Father who is crazy in love over you.

Sighting

(This is one of those ubiquitous Internet stories that come unattributed, although it is supposed to have been reported in a "southern newspaper." However, since I have heard this tale [with variations of course] at least fifty times during the years that I was broadcasting and writing about the dreadful phenomenon of sexual child abuse and consequently working with survivors, I include this sighting, convinced by the testimony of so many of its representative truth.)

An atheist couple raised their child in a godless home. The daughter had never heard about church, about Christ or about a heavenly father. One night when the little girl was five years old, the parents fought violently with each other, and the father took a gun and shot the mother. Then he turned the gun on himself and pulled the trigger.

This all happened in the presence of the horrified child.

The traumatized girl was placed in a Christian foster home. When the foster mother took the little girl to Sunday school, she told the teacher that the girl had never heard of Jesus, was in great pain and to have patience with her.

During class the teacher held up an illustration of Jesus and said, "Does anyone know who this is?"

The orphaned child raised her hand and said, "I do. That's the man who was holding me so very close the night my parents died."

4

THE THRILL OF THE HUNT

But may all who seek you rejoice and be glad in you; may those who love your salvation always say, "Let God be exalted!"

PSALM 70:4

In 1998 the French archeologist Franck Goddio mounted an expedition in the Bay of Aboukir, hunting for two Egyptian cities, Menouthis and Herakleion, which ancient writings show used to exist at the mouth of the Nile. Employing a nuclear resonance magnetometer, an X-ray-like instrument dangling from the back of the boat, Goddio and his exploration team scanned the harbor, back and forth, back and forth, making a map of the sea floor.

To their delight the magnetometer patterned two wide areas that eventually yielded the sites of submerged buildings, temples, large fallen columns, sphinxes and clay jugs that once stored wine. In addition, stele fragments, written records, sculptures and statues were located along with abandoned gold coins and jewelry. All this archeological booty lies buried beneath two feet of sand and twenty-one feet of Mediterranean waters.

None of the coins found in Menouthis were minted after A.D. 740, which leads to speculations that whatever disaster destroyed the two cities occurred sometime soon after this date. Whatever catastrophe swamped the cities—earthquakes or flooding or a combination of both—the archeological records of those civilizations has been preserved for a later generation of historical specialists to uncover and analyze.

There are mysteries that exist in the historical evidence beneath the sea or beneath the earth. The thrill of mounting expeditions, digging down through archeological tells, sounding the waters, piecing together the evidence to reveal the causes, discovering the patterns of ancient civilizations and determining the rise, decline and fall of empires has tantalized hunters for centuries.

Consequently scavengers scour the oceans looking for ancient shipwrecks with unplundered treasures. The sea hides plenty of submerged sailing vessels with much of their cargo intact. The Encyclopedia of Australian Shipwrecks contains over ten thousand entries. The hunt for drowned treasure is so intense, "The Abandoned Shipwreck Act of 1987" clarifies to which states boats discovered in which waters belong and how their archeological, historic and monetary values should be distributed and managed.

DISCOVERING THE THRILL

No matter what is being scavenged, an endemic hunting instinct dwells in each human; there is a thrill to finding something we have been seeking. Everyone loves to find that something special. The younger generations boast about what they have bought or sold on eBay. Financiers brag about "beating the stock market." Three high-school teachers I know devote many Saturdays and vacation days scanning beaches with radar devices, looking for treasure. And when we have been hunting for something in particular (a new dress or a new car), and we finally purchase it for a good price, we just have to tell somebody.

The thrill of the hunt can drive us to spend hours searching for that special find, as my oldest son, Randall, does when birdwatching. One September morning he invited me to go with him on a bird walk with the Du Page Birding Club. Along the way we heard the cry of a yellow-billed cuckoo and sighted many other species—two roosting black-crowned night herons, lots of catbirds, a few red-eyed vireos, a handful of warblers and dozens of cedar waxwings sunning in the trees.

No matter what it is you are seeking—treasures on the ocean's floor, designer labels in a resale shop, rare birds in the lofty treetops, pennies in the grass, the contents of a list for a teenager's scavenger hunt, wildflowers in a spring woods or first editions in a used book store—there is a thrill when you find it. That same delicious anticipation, that same excitement should be present when we hunt for God. Are you excited about what you might find? Let me ask this another way: Are you staying awake to God? "But we who would be born again indeed," writes George Mac-Donald, "must wake our souls unnumbered times a day."

Let us discover again the thrill of hunting for God, a most profitable activity with eternal consequences. Let us face our lives in the right direction. Let us look for him in the four ways that we have discovered are so helpful in the finding, the first of which is any obvious answer to prayer.

ANSWERS TO PRAYER

All of us make requests to God; the spiritual disconnect for humans rests in the fact that once we have achieved our heart's desire, we forget how frequently we pled with God for an answer. Barely tossing off a thank you, merrily we roll along. "See God anywhere around here recently?" someone asks. "Nope," we reply. "Don't think I did, now that you mention it."

One of my long-term prayer requests has been for help in making gardens around our house. We are surrounded by trees, the soil when we moved here was a thick clay streak, and I am an erratic gardener who can't stand mosquitoes and hates hot weather. Needless to say, I needed a great deal of help to create the fertile gardens I dreamed about, so I laid my request before God day after day, gardening season after gardening season. And he answered my prayer in his own timing, in a strange but obvious way.

Several autumn seasons back, septic leakage—smelly and foul—began to leak from the buried tank outside our back door, over which some bright contractor had poured a concrete patio. I consulted with three septic field services and received different recommendations for redress from all of them, with estimates ranging from $1,800 to $15,000. "Need the septic field map," said one service person. So I made inquiry phone calls, trekked over to the building division of the health department and procured a copy of the field that had been laid twenty-three years before.

"Not much help," said another septic field contractor. He waved the map beneath the nose of a coworker. "Couldn't get by with a sketch like this, could we? No, siree. Who'd you say put this in for you?" By this time I realized that part of septic field ethos is the disparagement of the skills and ethics of other services.

It was October by then, and I was enormously frustrated. Realizing that all decisions for septic fields came under my deployment as home administrator, I researched in several books how septic systems functioned and breathed some serious prayers for help, and when I called a fourth service, my questions were much more educated. They came to my house, dug a few holes, desecrated the patio garden, upturned the river-stone path, recommended I call the health department and charged me $125 for a consultation fee.

The health department in the complex of Du Page County office buildings is not open on Saturdays, so I interrupted weekday work to catch their personnel. "Can you help me? I've consulted with four services, and they all tell me the lines are dry, but one says that jetting the lines doesn't do any good. I should hook into the town sewer conduits. Another says I probably need a whole new septic field."

A representative from the health department came out, observed my septic pond (which I hoped was by then fertilizing the patio garden soil), and most helpful, gave me some names of nearby septic services the department would recommend. He told me I needed to get it fixed.

It was now December, and we were experiencing amazingly mild weather. One day the temperature spiked at around seventy degrees—in Chicago! I quickly called Black Gold, my service of choice, and asked if they could possibly get someone out to look at this mess. They promised to come the next day—the very day Chicago survived a twenty-two-inch snow dump, the second greatest in recorded history.

When we encountered another mild spell in February, I called Black Gold again and made sure I mentioned that I had consulted with the health department (figuring they would understand that I could also complain to the health department). A crew came out that warm afternoon, the yard was duly prodded with rods, an analysis of possible problems was determined, eight more deep holes were hand dug, an estimation for services-to-be-rendered was fixed, and they raced to get the work done before the next freeze and snowfall.

This time they carefully explained the procedures to me, and I discovered that this crew would do what the first septic service—the one that charged me some $3,000—should have done twenty-some years before, and what the contractor should have overseen when the house was built. They repaired the tacky job on the original field. I had plenty of dry line to absorb the septic waste; it just never had been connected!

When I came home from work that night, I was relieved that someone had finally eliminated our septic leakage in a way my instincts told me was a good job, but I was disheartened over the ruined back lawn and my destroyed garden! The plants had disappeared, and the clay bed was back on top.

My gloomy feelings lasted for a few days, but then I began to think, *Weren't there some opportunities in this as well?* Since an old oak had died the spring before my septic flood, the summer preceding this incident I had sun falling on my patio. Couldn't I now have a kitchen garden by the back door? Couldn't we have good dirt dumped

I bought eighteen dozen tulip bulbs and six boxes of crocuses at a clearance at Menards toward the end of October, but the fall was so busy that I didn't have a chance to plant them. However, God gave us one warm weekend in December, so I hung greens outside, coiled the garden hoses, turned over the garden pots, swept the front porch, clipped the dried artemesia for winter arrangements and planted all the bulbs in a wan sunshine that nevertheless felt so warm on my back I removed my jacket. It also melted the hoarfrost that had been forming on the earth, making the garden soil friable for my delayed planting.

on the west side of the lawn where I knew septic tiles no longer would be broken by heavy tires and loads? Couldn't I finally create a shade garden there over the new septic (actually the original) line?

This septic upheaval seemed like a drastic way to go about getting the gardens I had longed to have. But now three years

later I have finished the patio garden, rebuilt the soil above the
original lines and planted a shade bed, and I am ready to trans-
plant all the peony bushes into one spot to begin a spring garden. Obviously, with some retrospective vision, this was an answer to my prayers.

We find God intervening in our everyday world in any obvious
answers to prayer, but over the course of the long stories of our
lives, it is easy to forget that we prayed and God answered. The
temptation always exists not to see God's hand—back-hoeing my
hard clay, extending the beds, forcing me to build really good top-
soil, not to take shortcuts.

T. S. Eliot poses a series of questions in "Choruses from the
Rock" that bear on our finding God in the accumulated activities
and desires of our busy lives.

> The endless cycle of idea and action,
> Endless invention, endless experiment,
> Brings knowledge of motion, but not of stillness;
> Knowledge of speech, but not of silence;
> Knowledge of words, and ignorance of the Word,
> All our knowledge brings us nearer to our ignorance,
> All our ignorance brings us nearer to death,
> But nearness to death no nearer to God.
> Where is the Life we have lost in living?
> Where is the wisdom we have lost in knowledge?
> Where is the knowledge we have lost in information?

Where is God in the busyness of your days? Where is God answering your prayers (sometimes in obvious ways, sometimes in
slow and unfolding ways) that you have been overlooking in the
very motion of your life? Stop for a while, still yourself and seek
the answer to this question.

EVIDENCE OF HIS CARE

The second category for finding God is through any unexpected evidence of his care. As illustration, I offer another story out of my life.

One December afternoon while driving home from work I went to sleep at the wheel, a little unintended nap totaling about $3,500 worth of damage to the front end of my new Ford Escort. I was rudely wakened with that terrible sound of metal crunching against metal. *Oh, no!* I thought. *I've hit the trailer van ahead of me!*

But as we pulled over to the side of the road, I immediately felt surrounded by protective good. The truck pulling the trailer bore an imprint of a nearby farm on its side panel, and the driver, a Cuban immigrant who worked for the farm, showed his concern as he inquired about my condition. *What a soft, gentle smile,* I thought. Instead of justifiable road rage, I was granted tenderness.

"I'm OK," I replied. "But I am so sorry. I must have gone to sleep at the wheel. This is all my fault."

We both examined my car's crumpled front end. I felt grateful to have walked away apparently undamaged. The other driver assured me he was fine, but it looked as though the impact had jammed the tongue of the trailer out of the couplings and the couplings off the back of the truck.

A Winfield Township service car pulled over to the shoulder of the road. "Everyone OK?" the driver called. "I've got a cell phone," he said. "And I know the owner of Janesway Farms." The township worker proceeded to phone both the police and the owner of the farm, and within minutes they had arrived.

"You OK?" asked the Du Page County Sheriff from the front seat of his marked police car. We showed our licenses through the window as we recounted the accident. I volunteered culpability. To my surprise no moving violation was issued.

"Hey! I know you," said James Joy, the owner of Janesway Farms. Our families had gone to church together long ago, and our youth group used to take hayrides from the barn on the homestead, which once bordered County Farm Road. "Are you sure you're OK?" he inquired.

Soon the men tested my engine, checked if it would start, and it did. They opened and closed the driver's door to see if it still worked, found a bungee cord and hooked the now-corrugated hood to the bumper. We all noticed the black damp spot of leaking liquid. "Probably transmission fluid," James Joy said. "But it'll get you home."

Driving home, I realized with an inner chill that if the trailer had not been directly in front of me, I might have shot across the highway and collided with an oncoming vehicle, and although I was shaken, and the next day achingly sore, I was OK. I began to piece together the unexpected evidence of God's care. His love had been all around me during and after the accident.

I must admit that there are often times when I am tempted to believe I do more for God than he does for me. Ever feel the same? Ministry can consume me. I've given everything I've got to give. The problems are unending. When is God going to keep his promises? I have been praying for some things for five years, for ten years, even twenty years. Is God on a retreat of silence?

And then, when danger occurs, it is as though God's unseen good cannot constrain itself. These incidents, if we recognize the divine protection in them, begin to convince us that God is active on our behalf. We become suddenly aware (if we are attending) to the fact that the unseen "real" is bending toward us with unusual love. God rushes forward, trespassing the boundaries he himself has ordained between the material and the supernatural. Solace quickly, overwhelmingly, surrounds us. *Are you OK? Are you*

OK? During these moments of unexpected evidence of his care, we remember he is working on our behalf, that the omnipotent muteness we have been experiencing is mostly because we don't hear very well, not because God isn't talking.

Because of a strong commitment to racial reconciliation, we began attending Second Baptist Church, the oldest black congregation in Du Page County, Illinois. This was during a long wilderness passage in our lives, and daily, if not weekly, we considered closing our ministry and declaring bankruptcy. However, as long as we owed creditors, we felt we needed to stay the course as long as possible.

Almost every Sunday the Word came to us from our black brothers and sisters. It was given in the sermons, in the music, in testimony. The Word spoke to us: "Don't give up," "God will see you through," "Hold on," "Don't jump the ship," "Don't turn back," "Keep on going." It is one thing to hear a godly message that reaches the soul every now and then, but it is another thing to hear the same message Sunday after Sunday for several years! If you don't listen to that Word, you are a fool. We stuck with it.

God's care is in the basics, in the usual evidences of his care that we take for granted (then we have the gall to complain that we can't see him working on our behalf). The African American church where David and I attend has a litany of thanksgiving they pray Sunday after Sunday: "Thank you that we woke up this morning in our right minds, that we have food on the table, clothes on our backs, shoes on our feet, a roof over our head, and a job to go to." His care is everywhere, but sometimes we need a shaking up to realize it again.

During the Christmas season after my car accident, disabled slightly due to soreness, I thought more deeply about the Scripture from Luke, "And there were shepherds living out in the fields nearby, keeping watch over their flocks at night. An angel of the Lord appeared to them, and the glory of the Lord shone around them, and they were terrified" (Luke 2:8-9). I'd always thought of a band of angel hosts shimmering in the sky startling enough, but I'd been told that the word used in the Scripture implies that the angels were among the shepherds, down on the ground, all around them in a more immediate way. No wonder they were terrified. "The glory of the Lord shone around them."

Oh, we long for that. We want to see that glory and to listen to angelic choirs. We yearn to hear the hosts proclaim peace on earth, goodwill to mankind. And I want the peaceable kingdom to come soon, that kingdom where the swords and guns are turned into plowshares. If all this would happen, I would really know that God was interested in my life. I have a preference for short prayers, quickly answered, in spectacular sorts of ways. But I wake up in my right mind each morning, I have food on the table, clothes on my back, shelter over my head and a job to go to. A bounty of evidences of God's care enfolds me.

Indeed, the love of the Lord is all around me whether I recognize it or not. It breaks through in unaccountable moments, often when we are in danger; it rushes forth to be "grounded" with us. It is substantive, concrete, tangible, comprehensible, giving practical testament to his sustaining compassion.

I fell asleep while driving my car one December afternoon and rear-ended the vehicle ahead of me. But I'm OK (I just remembered again). The Lord is all around me.

How are you seeing any unexpected evidence of God's care?

HELP TO DO GOD'S WORK

The third category in which we can choose to see God intervening on our behalf is any help to do God's work in the world. Initially people often have difficulty understanding this category, so allow me to state that it is not only people in professional ministry who are helped to do God's work in the world. Every Christian is God's representative. Whenever we do something that brings forth good, that stands for what is just, honest and true, that witnesses to his love, that shares the good news of the gospel, we have been helped to do God's work in the world.

For example, a woman spends a morning cooking, makes two casseroles, one for the freezer and one for the table. A phone call comes telling of an emergency in another household; the frozen casserole goes out the door as a gift of charity and concern.

Someone writes a note, someone drops past a hospital room. Young fathers take care of six children combined, all under the age of eight, so their wives can spend an evening together enjoying their friendship without the urgent interruptions of offspring. A crippled senior and her friend make up packages of treats to distribute in their retirement complex's nursing center. A Sunday school class organizes and conducts a protest march at a proposed abortion clinic. Internationals are invited for dinner. Children who have been abused are adopted into a family. Volunteers clean the church kitchen, stuff letters for a not-for-profit, travel overseas and donate medical expertise. All this, and thousands of other unnamed deeds of kindness, are God's work set loose into the world. Recognizing his help to do this work is part of the God Hunt.

One afternoon in January the desk phone rang in my office. "Hello," said an unfamiliar voice, "This is Sears Maintenance Agreements. What size is your refrigerator?"

"Who—what?" I stammered, surprised. "My refrigerator? It's a side-by-side, but . . . I'm in my office, and I really don't know what size it is." Then I remembered that last year when a representative from Sears called, inquiring as to whether I wanted to take out a maintenance agreement on any appliance of my choice, I took a calculated risk and put out $125 to cover my eleven-year-old refrigerator. (The icemaker had been repaired countless times. With my appliance man retiring and moving to Florida, the chances of it breaking again were pretty good. Sure enough, in a month the icemaker went kaput, and over the Christmas season a repairman visited my kitchen on three separate occasions. No results.)

The voice on the office phone continued, "Well, we can't repair the icemaker in your Amana. The manufacturer no longer makes that part. Sears will stand by its agreement and replace your refrigerator with a comparative model up to $900. Please go to your nearby Sears store and pick out a new one."

"A whole new refrigerator?" I gasped. I would have been happy with a few new plastic ice cube trays. Yes, the woman assured me, a whole new refrigerator.

Before the benevolent climate could take a sudden turn for the worse, I immediately checked out consumer guides, determined which brand and model was highly ranked, did some comparison shopping, then marked when the next sales started at Sears. Sure enough, one Saturday afternoon I hurried to the mall and found the exact model I had decided on (no icemaker, a low freezer compartment, refrigerator unit on top, sliding shelves, great door space, super organization and excellent energy savings). The sale price was exactly $899!

I decided to donate the old refrigerator (perfectly good except for a faulty icemaker) to replace the one in the kitchen at work, which was in bad shape. But in order to make the side-by-side fit, we needed to move stuff—the pop machine, for instance—and ditch the too-small old refrigerator. The staff and I decided that

My son and I were in Milan over the Christmas season, and all the restaurants recommended in our guidebooks were closed. We were getting weary with the walking. In frustration we finally stopped and asked directions from a stranger sitting on a stoop. (Jeremy speaks fluent Spanish and Mandarin and had studied enough to develop a working tourist Italian.)

"Where can we find a decent restaurant that is open and not too costly?" Jeremy asked in broken Italian. Lo and behold, the man, who was waiting for his wife, was from Ecuador. When his wife came, they walked eight blocks with us to the Metro, Jeremy chattering away with them in Spanish. They showed us how to buy inexpensive holiday passes, rode with us to our stop (making sure we knew how to get back), got off at the Cathedral Plaza where there were many eateries, and then walked with us, pointing out good dining places that were open and not too costly!

junk had accumulated in the kitchen. Out with the old computer manuals! No need for those rusty metal shelves! Move the mail-stuffing apparatus that crowded the kitchen to a newly appointed mailroom! Take the unused desk and dividers out of the new mailroom and distribute them around the rest of the office! Get rid of the ugly vintage 1950s desks and the battered furniture we no longer needed! Paint the kitchen! And as long as we were reorganizing, shouldn't we clean and vacuum and scrub everything else?

One act encourages another. Room is made for people when accumulated junk gets trashed. Something gets moved, and we find the dust and dirt beneath and behind it. Cleaning begins. Generosity is given; generosity is given away. This is the way with God's good gifts given through us into the world. We know it is God by the timing, by the appropriateness, by the depth of impact and by the way it goes on having good effects, multiplying itself in unaccountable ways.

How is God helping you to do his work in the world?

UNUSUAL LINKAGE OR TIMING

The fourth category in the God Hunt is any unusual linkage or timing. Linkage and timing are those grand designs when something happens at just the right moment—exactly when it is needed. The human tendency is to respond, "What a coincidence!" I will reiterate the words of Graham Hess in the film *Signs*, "There are no coincidences. Someone is watching out for you."

Perhaps the best place we can see unusual linkage and timing is in the stories

The darkest time in the year,

The poorest place in the town,

Cold, and a taste of fear,

Man and woman alone,

What can we hope for here?

More light than we can learn,

More wealth than we can treasure,

More love than we can earn,

More peace than we can measure,

Because one Child is born.

—Christopher Fry

from the scriptural accounts where the long, involved intervention of the divine has been condensed to just a few passages. From the beginning of human history God was plotting a master design that was titled "Redemption." He created the world and the creatures, designed a garden, breathed life into man and woman, blessed it all for its goodness and became intimate with his creation. They, of course, sinned, and soon God began to work his scheme out through a nation called Israel; this was a strategy nonpareil that took centuries to engineer. Forewarnings, prophecies and sage predictions gave glimmers of this divine stratagem:

> A shoot will come up from the stump of Jesse;
>> from his roots a Branch will bear fruit.
> The Spirit of the LORD will rest on him—
>> the Spirit of wisdom and of understanding,
>> the Spirit of counsel and of power,
>> the Spirit of knowledge and of the fear of the LORD.
> (Isaiah 11:1-2)

Only when everything was perched precipitously, when it was exquisitely ready, did God carry out his plan.

> But when the time had fully come, God sent his Son, born of a woman, born under law, to redeem those under law, that we might receive the full rights of sons. Because you are sons, God sent the Spirit of his Son into our hearts, the Spirit who calls out, *"Abba,* Father." So you are no longer a slave, but a son; and since you are a son, God has made you also an heir. (Galatians 4:4-7)

Then the divine stratagem continues. God is now manifest on earth in the flesh of his Son, Jesus Christ. A quote of uncertain origin copied into my prayer journal captures this succinctly: "Jesus

is God spelling himself out in language that man can understand."
A genius dramaturge, Christ orchestrates the ongoing acts of this
master design. Not until the exact moment does he give himself
up to the hands of his executioners. The stars in the heaven, the
dates on the calendar, the actors and players, the world power
politics, the staging, the lighting, the curtain parting, the death,
the dying, burial and resurrection; climax, dénouement, conclu-
sion—it was all in his hands.

Do you really think the amazing things that happen in your life
are circumstances? No. No. No. It is unusual linkage and timing.
Someone, someone who loves you, is working on your behalf.

THE ETERNAL THRILL

The thrill of the hunt, finding possible riches, can lead men and
women to devote themselves to fruitless ventures that have little
tangible rewards. One of the longest treasure hunts in the world
began in 1795 on Oak Island in Mahone Bay, Nova Scotia, when
a boy noticed a curious depression in the ground, above which
stood a huge oak tree with a sawed-off branch. Like anybody else
with an ounce of adventure in his soul, this young boy—and two
eager friends—began to dig.

Just two feet down the boys came upon a strange layer of
stones, and later, at ten, twenty and thirty feet, they discovered
platforms of carefully fitted oak logs—evidence of a shaft that
showed skillful engineering. But who had dug it and why?

The three friends pursued the puzzle into adulthood, finally
having to find financial backing. Their digging uncovered more
log platforms every ten feet to a depth of ninety feet, as well as
layers of charcoal, putty and coconut fiber—although no one
could explain what coconut fiber was doing on a rain-chilled island fifteen hundred miles from the closest coconut palm.

Then even stranger things began to happen as their shovels hit a large, flat stone inscribed in a strange code, which a scholar claimed to translate: "Ten feet below are two million pounds buried."

One morning when the diggers arrived at the pit, they found the shaft flooded with seawater. By digging deeper they'd triggered an ingenious booby trap that opened two flooding tunnels, one of which still runs to old Smuggler's Cove, on the east end of Oak Island, where investigations in 1850 revealed a man-made beach which contained a network of stone-lined channels that led right into the pit. Thus, to reach the presumed treasure hunters would first have the awesome chore of bailing out the Atlantic Ocean.

Men have since brought in pumps, cranes, drilling rigs and power shovels. In or near the shaft, they've discovered scissors of Mexican origin, pieces of wire that tests show were made prior to 1750 and links of gold chain. Near the shore, searchers have found a triangle of stones that points directly to the treasure pit.

The latest treasure hunter trying to solve the compelling puzzle of Oak Island is a man named Dan Blankenship, who has been digging in the pit for twenty-one years; he's now backed by a businessman's group that has sunk over one million dollars into digging. "That's why we call it the Money Pit," Dan jokes. "We've found archeological artifacts, but nothing you can put in the bank." And each week the shaft numbered 10-X gets four feet deeper, four feet closer to—well, who knows?

All this is motivated not only by a search for money, but also by the thrill of the hunt. The God Hunt can evoke the same thrill of finding, but it is immensely, deeply satisfying to the soul, "Oh, the depth of the riches of the wisdom and knowledge of God!" writes Paul in Romans 11:33. "How unsearchable his judgments, and his paths beyond tracing out!"

However, Paul promises that the spiritual treasure hunts on which Christians embark will be fulfilled. This hunt will not be a fruitless endeavor or a financially draining Money Pit.

For this reason I kneel before the Father. . . . I pray that out of his glorious riches he may strengthen you with power through his Spirit in your inner being, so that Christ may dwell in your hearts through faith. And I pray that you, being rooted and established in love, may have power, together with all the saints, to grasp how wide and long and high and deep is the love of Christ, and to know this love that surpasses knowledge. (Ephesians 3:14-19)

The eternal thrill of the hunt is found in the seeking and finding of God in this world—any obvious answer to prayer, any unexpected evidence of his care, any help to do his work in the world, any unusual linkage and timing. May we all be able to pray this prayer:

Christ, you came into the world not as one sent from God, nor as one who knew God, but as God himself hurrying to save us. How can we help but run to you? No one else has shown us such great love. Amen.

Sighting

Tammi Conn shares a God Hunt sighting that is a classic example of linkage and timing.

I graduated from Southern Illinois University in December of 1996. I tried to stay in Carbondale but could not get a job. So I finally gave up the job hunt and moved home in November of 1998. I worked at a travel company but wasn't happy there, since as a secretary I wasn't using my degree in business education. I sent out résumés to three local high schools and to the Evangelical Training Association (ETA). ETA responded and hired me. The high schools sent applications, but since I had a job I didn't fill any of them out.

I started at ETA in February of 1999, and I enjoyed the challenge of the job. At the end of July, however, I received a message from Geneva High School that the business teacher had resigned. They had received my résumé from Hinsdale South High School. Since I had promised

ETA at least a year of service, I wasn't actively pursuing a place in education, but since I knew I wanted to teach on the high school level, I went to the interview (for the experience), was called back, but wasn't hired (more experience).

About two weeks later I got a call from Kaneland High School. Their business teacher had quit, leaving a position to fill. Apparently the résumé that I sent to Hinsdale South was faxed to Geneva in July 1999, then faxed to Kaneland in August of 1999.

I thought about the disadvantages of waiting another year to start a career in my chosen profession during the forty-five-minute drive out to Kaneland and decided that I would take the position if it was offered, provided it was at a salary of at least $25,000. The interview was grueling, but I was offered the position on the spot for $26,500.

To end up with a good position at ETA and then to be sought after for a position in my chosen field could have been the result of my moving back North. But the résumé that lived from February 1999 to August 1999 was definitely the work of the Lord!

5

TRAIL SIGNS

There is another world and it is in this one.

PAUL ELUARD

One winter in an attempt to enjoy the great outdoors even in the cold, I ordered a prize-winning video for the grandchildren indecorously titled *Trail Signs: Poop, Paws, and Footprints*. Bundled up in winter woolens and almost ready for our trek, I first watched the how-to video with my two grandchildren, ages five and three. To my surprise the narrator taught us how to track brown bear, caribou, moose and ocelots—none of which I recall having ever seen around the western suburbs of Chicago. I had been thinking more of identifying the droppings and prints of rabbits, raccoons, dogs, groundhogs, possums and an occasional deer.

However, we made the most of it. We plodded beneath the sun and in the snow along the path, sighted nests in bare trees, found a dead bird and followed many unidentified but certainly important signs—until our feet became really cold and we went home to make hot chocolate in a warm kitchen.

Learning to read trail signs—poop, paws and footprints—is one of the basic faculties of hunting. Not long after my mind had been focused toward tracking love, I received additional instructions. While sharing meals together in the dining hall of Gospel for Asia Biblical Seminary outside the city of Tiruvalla in southern India, I discovered that the Gospel for Asia website manager, John Schwartz, was an avid sportsman.

"There have to be rules that every good hunter learns to follow," I started, knowing I had brought work to do on the God Hunt.

The young man's eyes lighted. "Absolutely," he replied.

"What are some of them?" I asked, not believing my good fortune at having an avid hunting expert at hand.

"Well, let's see . . . you always want to go upwind. By that I mean the wind needs to be blowing into your face. If it blows from behind you, the animals will smell you and run." By this time, I had my notebook out and was jotting copious notes.

John continued by explaining that it was also important to know the nature of the species I might be hunting. "For instance," said my new hunting friend, "if you are hunting bear, you look up in the sky for seagulls. Seagulls always follow bears and eat the scraps they leave behind. Or if you are duck hunting, and you are waiting in a blind for a flyover, you want to be totally camouflaged. During a flyover you must keep perfectly still—don't even look up; the birds will see that movement." Some of this was applicable. As already mentioned, bears in my neighborhood are few—but ducks—well, we have hundreds of Canada geese around Chicago. That counted, certainly.

"You also want to be fit and trim so you can bring out your kill," John said. "If you are trekking across hard country, uphill and down, in mountainous terrain or moving through thick underbrush, the travel with the equipment you carry in and the carcasses you carry out can be pretty arduous. So in the months before you go hunting, you want to take on some disciplined training." (Later I read a report from the Department of Environmental Conservation, a division of Fish, Wildlife, and Marine

Resources, noting that heart attacks during the hunting season take a higher toll than careless hunting practices. "Get physically fit," the bulletin recommended. "Physical fitness will enable you to cover more ground when hunting, get your game out of the woods easier and avoid clumsiness and dangerous lapses of concentration and caution that accompany exhaustion.")

"Oh, yes," John continued, thinking of other rules off the top of his head. "Prepare the carcass the right way and do it right away. Make sure you take the equipment you will need to hunt and what you will need for your own survival." He paused to tell a hunter's story of novice gunmen who did not follow some of these rules and who were dangerous in the field. Then he resumed listing rules. "Never shoot more than the limit or more than you can prepare. Always follow the published hunter's regulations (the same goes for fishermen). Some species can only be hunted in certain seasons, and there may be a limit on what you can bag. Learn to walk quietly and be still. Make sure you know how to stop, drop and roll."

My conversation with John was enlightening, and when I returned home from India and visited Internet sites on hunting, I discovered even more. Hunting regulations are extensive, particular to each state and country, and have a primary goal, not just of safety, but of wildlife conservation. Everything about hunting is regulated. No matter what species you're hunting or what method you're using, you must have a hunting license. In order to qualify for a license, you must take the required courses that teach respect for public and private property, develop wildlife identification skills, learn to use appropriate weapons and begin training in conservation appreciation.

The lists of lawful and unlawful hunting methods (with the resulting penalties) are posted, accessible to all, and are pages long.

On a sample site, that of the Virginia Department of Game and
Inland Fisheries, I found regulations so precise as to delineate
where and how hunting could be conducted by counties, ranges
and boundaries (West of the Blue Ridge, for example, and East of
the Blue Ridge in Bedford, Fairfax, Franklin, Henry Loudoun,
Northampton and Patrick Counties, and so on).

*One of my great difficulties in life is being able to find
handymen we can afford. My husband is not a home
improvement guru, and I have limited capacities in household
repair. We had an outside outlet that was not working, so I
couldn't plug in Christmas lights or power lawn equipment. I'd
asked for workmen to fix this, but they had always overlooked
my request. One morning as I was cleaning out a drawer, a
business card fell to the floor. It reminded me that a friend
had told me her husband was doing freelance electrical work
while she was attending seminary. I made the phone call and
that morning he came over, fixed my outlet and charged me
$50, an amount I was able and willing to pay.*

There are regulations for hunting with dogs, for training dogs,
for following and retrieving hunting dogs. There are regulations
on when and where a hunter can hunt bobcat during deer season
or foxes during deer season. There are specialized tagging requirements for kills, and there are wildlife checkpoints to make
sure regulations are followed. There are sunrise-sunset time-
tables directing hunting hours ("One-half hour before sunrise to

one-half hour after sunset for nonmigratory birds and game except during spring gobbler season, etc.")

I was fascinated. Every hunting category, from stamp collecting to fungi identification (the hunter needs to know which toadstools are poisonous) has its own rules. In addition, extensive collecting and gathering subcultures exist for exchanging information, or for forming associations and memberships. For example, enter the search word *philatelic,* which has to do with the collection and study of postage stamps, on the Web, or look at one of the 24,300 references that pop up for the category of "mushroom hunters."

Doesn't finding God in our everyday world have some rules of its own as well? Perhaps we should call them principles, ways that assist us in better recognizing the divine as it interfaces with the human. In my experience the first principle of hunting God is, *What you are seeking is closer than you think.*

CONTINUALLY AND ETERNALLY PRESENT

Before the time of Moses, God's revelations of his identity to the patriarchs concerned promises belonging to a distant future. The name by which they knew him (El Shaddai or God Almighty) presupposed that he was competent to fulfill his future promises. The revelation at the burning bush was greater and more intimate. It was a promise of immediacy, of holy presence, of the One who is always being in our moment, of One in whom there is a past and present and future all at once.

Strictly speaking, the "I AM" that God breathed out to Moses from the site of the burning bush was the only name of God. It is written YHWH (pronounced Yahweh), but is considered so holy to Jewish people that it is not spoken out loud by them. After Moses' return to Egypt, God says, "I am the LORD [YHWH]. I appeared to Abraham, to Isaac and to Jacob as God Almighty, but by my name the LORD [YHWH] I did not make myself known to them" (Exodus 6:2-3).

This name, I AM, makes a covenant that God is with his people. It is a revelation of God's true identity and indicates an expectation that the people who knew his esoteric and holy name would fashion their private and national lives differently than the societies around them.

When Jesus comes to earth he affirms his connection with the Father by using the name I AM. In John 4 the Samaritan woman at the well says to Jesus, "I know that Messiah is coming. When he comes, he will explain everything to us" (v. 25). Jesus responds, "I who speak to you am he," declaring that he was the fulfillment of all Israel's religious and national yearnings (v. 26).

Again Christ links himself to the Old Testament revelation when the Jews challenge his authority. John 8 records the dramatic, heated confrontation between Jesus and the Jews who were seeking to kill him.

> The Jews answered him, "Aren't we right in saying that you are a Samaritan and demon-possessed?"
>
> "I am not possessed by a demon," said Jesus, "but I honor my Father and you dishonor me. . . . I tell you the truth, if anyone keeps my word, he will never see death."
>
> At this the Jews exclaimed, "Now we know that you are demon-possessed! Abraham died. . . . Are you greater than our father Abraham? He died, and so did the prophets. Who do you think you are?" (vv. 48-52)

At this point the spiritual universe bent close, hushed itself and waited with bated breath for the enormous pronouncement. "'I tell you the truth,' Jesus answered. 'Before Abraham was born,

I AM'" (John 8:58, emphasis added). And what he uttered was so shocking to the Jewish mind that the challengers took up stones to throw at him. In their minds this young upstart had just uttered blasphemy; he had claimed to be God. But this is more than a statement of existence, more than a description of identity; it is the King of the Universe taking off his beggar's disguise and revealing himself as the royal heir apparent. "I AM THAT I AM," cried the voice from the burning bush, and Christ revealed himself with the same words, "Before Abraham was born, I AM."

This YHWH is the coordinating arc between the two canons. Among many Scriptures, the apostle Paul verifies this in a Colossians passage, "He is the image of the invisible God, the firstborn of all creation, for in him all things were created, in heaven and on earth, visible and invisible, whether thrones or dominions or principalities or authorities. . . . He is before all things, and in him all things hold together. He is the head of the body, the church; he is the beginning, the firstborn from the dead, that in everything he might be pre-eminent" (Colossians 1:15-18 RSV). Notice that, again, the present tense dominates.

All the "I am" statements of Christ refer back to the remarkable encounter between a craggy-faced, desert-blasted nomad named Moses and the God who declared himself as YHWH from a scraggy bush that flamed forth. I AM the Light of the world. I AM the bread. I AM the door. I AM the vine. I AM the good shepherd. I who AM speaking to you am he. I AM the Alpha and the Omega who is and was and who is to come, the Almighty. I AM the first and the last. I AM the resurrection and the life.

In these pronouncements Jesus is declaring that he is YHWH and expanding our understanding of the ineffable. John declares this in a different way in his written Gospel: "In the beginning was the Word, and the Word was with God, and the Word was God. He was with God in the beginning. Through him all things were made; without him nothing was made that has been made. In him was life, and that life was the light of men" (John 1:1-4). In short, John is saying that Christ is the I AM THAT I AM.

This has overwhelming bearings on our spiritual hunting. If we believe Christ declared himself to be the God who is continually and eternally present, and if we choose to rest in that reality, then it means that Jesus, through the Holy Spirit, is available, near us, ready to be heard, close at hand, working with us in this moment, in this day, in this month and in this year. Once this reality reaches our understanding, can any of us ever be the same?

The incarnation, which is way beyond my comprehension and which I refuse to even attempt to reduce to a paragraph of inadequate words, has to do with the I AM of God's infinitude intersecting with the I am of my finitude. This is the prophetic message made understandable to Joseph, the surrogate father of the infant Jesus. In a dream an angel explains that Joseph is to take Mary as wife, despite her pregnancy which he knew he had not incepted. "And you are to give him the name Jesus, because he will save his people from their sins" (Matthew 1:21). The writer, Matthew, makes a link, "All this took place to fulfill what the Lord had said through the prophet: 'The virgin will be with child and will give birth to a son, and they will call him 'Immanuel'—which means, 'God with us'" (Matthew 1:22-23).

Pardon me while I go and weep for the reality of this that is beyond my capacities to fully know. If I am not impacted emotionally and psychologically, if I do not stand stunned by blazing wonder, I must then examine if my actions display that I really believe this to be true. Or are all these declarations of God's presence only words printed in ink on parchment-like pages, the religious lore of centuries perpetuated by preachers and teachers, but without essential meaning?

Participating in the daily God Hunt, intentionally seeking to see God jump out and surprise me (at any time, in any moment), is the way I display that I believe this shattering announcement to be true, and living by it, I thereby mount a personal resistance that declares "I am not content to live a placidly nominal Christian life!" The first principle of the God Hunt—*What you are seeking is closer than you think*—is rooted in the incarnation of Christ and his declaration that he is God, YHWH, the I AM.

JESUS AMONG US

David and I recently experienced Christ's presence with us when we had the privilege of teaching a dedicated group of church leaders in India. While David taught a communication model that he had developed, I worked with the women seminarians during evening prayers, after dinner and before their library study. All these men and women spoke English, but the various accents and pronunciations, as well as the rotating fans in the lecture room, made hearing and understanding somewhat difficult. I began my first session by reminding them that although we spoke the same language, because I didn't understand all cultural nuances, I might say or do something that would be unintentionally offensive. "Forgive me if this happens. Know that my spirit is one of apology ahead of time. Please make allowances for my ignorance of your ways."

We needn't have worried. We were warmly received, and by the second day, after submitting themselves to sermon delivery and evaluation, they began to enculturate the model, then quickly started to devise a plan to teach it to all those pastors in the hundreds of churches for which they were responsible.

The weather was warm and humid, and I had packed a minimal amount of clothing, thinking I would purchase some Indian costumes if I had a chance to shop. On the third day our friends ran us into town and in a whirl of trying on garments, of translating sizes (I wear an extra-large in India), I found three sari outfits, the lovely long dresses with matching pants and shawls.

When I put on the sari outfit and wore it on campus, I suddenly sensed a heightened quality of approval and receptivity that was degrees above what we had already experienced. I was wearing their national garments. I had put on the clothes of their custom. Everyone commented, pleased. The women came closer and fingered the fabric. "That looks very good on you," they said. "Will you wear this when you go home?"

I said I probably would. And I have, using the outfit to demonstrate how our best friend Christ puts on our garments—our flesh. Jesus "became flesh and made his dwelling among us," writes John in John 1:14. Jesus wore our Punjabi outfit, the very flesh that we wear. In 1 John 1:1, when John writes, "That which was from the beginning, which we have heard, which we have seen with our eyes, which we have looked at and our hands have touched," I can imagine him thinking, *We have fingered his garments, pinching the fabric between the fingers, this flesh we have bumped against, skin against skin. We have touched, held and embraced his body. A manly bonhomie, a forthright jostling between buddies, has been evidence of our closeness and regard. This lithe form with which we have danced the circle of celebration at weddings and during Jewish high-festival days, bathed with and trudged with, this flesh has been with us, present to us, holding us and washing us and bleeding for us and suffering for us. This Jesus we declare unto you. We are witnesses of his incarnation, we have seen the I AM become human.* What a wonder!

SPIRITUAL TRAIL SIGNS

In the films *The Gods Must Be Crazy, Part I* and *Part II,* an enchanting contrast is built between the illiteracy of people today regarding the ways of the deep Kalahari of Africa and the sophisticated tracking knowledge of the Bushman, Xixo. "In the morning they like to read the news," the narrator says, as the tribe members bend over tracks in the earth. "The hyena has a new girlfriend; the cheetah has lost one of her babies; the orax is starting to migrate to the West."

In the second film, through a series of absurd incidents, Dr. Ann Taylor has been stranded in the wild, and the path of the white woman and the little man cross. Xixo observes that she is quite illiterate—she can't read any of the trail signs in the ground.

Like Dr. Taylor in this film, we are too often illiterate regarding spiritual trail signs. We have not been taught to hunt for God in the everyday, yet all we need to do is ask, Has the tracking God crossed my path in any tangible way today?

The patriarchs, kings and prophets encountered the living God in the Old Testament. Commoners, men and women of ordinary means, children, slaves, wives and husbands knew moments impregnated with the holy. The New Testament world experienced God in the flesh, through Christ. Now we, today, can experience God in the everyday through the gift of the Holy Spirit, the Spirit of truth, the very Spirit of Jesus who works to make himself knowable within our own souls and comprehensible as he intervenes in the commonplace around us. As we search for God in the everyday, the Holy Spirit enlightens the Scriptures when we look to them. Our physical eyes are given the gift of seeing the nature of God in the created world around us, and our spiritual sight is enabled so we can observe him working in the daily incidents, both good and bad, that he can make meaningful if we allow it.

FINDING WHAT WAS LOST

In the Gospels, Christ tells many hunting stories. There are so many, I have come to conclude that hunting and finding are important to him. There are the stories of the lost son and of the lost sheep. There are stories about the hiddenness of the kingdom of God: "The kingdom of heaven is like treasure hidden in a field. When a man found it, he hid it again, and then in his joy went and sold all he had and bought that field. Again, the kingdom of heaven is like a merchant looking for fine pearls. When he found one of great value, he went away and sold everything he had and bought it" (Matthew 13:44-45).

Many of these parables of lost things, of the hunting and finding of them, are clumped together as though the Teacher taught them in sequences. In Luke we have the parable of the lost sheep, the lost coin and the lost son, in that order, all in one chapter. I used to think this was because whoever compiled the Gospels organized the hunting stories into a category and filed it under "Lost Things." I'm beginning to suspect that Christ told the tales this way for effect. The three in Luke progress from the story of a lost animal, to a lost monetary treasure with sentimental value, to a lost human. That layering has the potential to bring listeners into a meaningful understanding.

"Suppose a woman has ten silver coins and loses one. Does she not light a lamp, sweep the house and search carefully until she finds it?" (Luke 15:8). The coin was from her wedding necklace, a customary gift of great value given to brides on their marriage day, a sign to the watching world of the pleasure placed in her by her bridegroom (or his family), and a kind of insurance should anything disastrous happen and her husband be unable to provide for her.

I can certainly relate to the urgency and determination of this woman to find the coin. Several years ago my husband, David, lost his wedding ring. It had grown a little tight (or through the years he had grown a little fat), and he would often slip it off his ring finger to his small finger. One day the ring fell off without David's knowledge. Like the woman in the parable, we searched our house from top to bottom. We looked in his study where he last remembered wearing the ring. We hunted under couch cushions and poked into the crevices of the sofa. We crawled around on our hands and knees, spying in corners and under furniture. Not a drawer was overlooked, not a pocket was ignored and not a storage box or crevice escaped our attention. Sadly we never found his wedding ring. Sentimentally inscribed "forever and always," it was lost forever.

Having experienced the loss of David's ring and the anxious hunt to find it, I could all too well understand the joy of the woman in the parable when she found her coin. "And when she finds it, she calls her friends and neighbors together and says, 'Rejoice with me; I have found my lost coin'" (Luke 15:9). If we had found David's wedding ring, I am certain I would have told some of my children with delight, "We found Daddy's ring! Guess where we found it?"

All of us have something valuable we have misplaced at some time in our lives—a pet that has run away perhaps, an item we cherished, important papers, or even a precious loved one. The hunts that we embark on to find these lost things help us understand the urgency behind the hunting stories in the New Testament: "Suppose one of you has a hundred sheep and loses one of them. Does he not leave the ninety-nine in the open country and go after the lost sheep until he finds it? And when he finds it, he joyfully puts it on his shoulders and goes home" (Luke 15:4-5).

Have you lost intimacy with the I AM THAT I AM? How long

has it been since you identified the ever present, potentially always imminent God who took on your garment, now made even more intimate by the indwelling Holy Spirit? Haven't you been restless somehow in your deepest soul? Aren't you uneasy, feeling that there must be something more? If so, you need to go trekking. You need to end this spiritual illiteracy and begin reading the signs on the ground that are all around you.

What you are seeking is closer than you think.

Sighting

Marian Oliver, Director of Product Resources at Mainstay Ministries, tells about a visit to the Wheaton Eye Clinic for a routine eye exam. Normally the clinicians check your vision, then dilate your pupils. On this occasion, however, the examiner, usually employed in the glaucoma section, was substituting in the examining rooms. Because Marian is farsighted, the examiner elected not to do the dilation because of a natural tendency to look out for glaucoma in farsighted people. Marian says that no one had ever delayed dilation before, and her vision had not changed much since her last appointment.

When the eye doctor saw Marian, he diagnosed an irregularity and said that if Marian's eyes had been dilated, she would have experienced an acute attack of closed-angle glaucoma on the spot with nausea, vomiting, severe pain, possible loss of vision and other complications. He immediately referred her to a glaucoma specialist who said that the canal in the eye that allows fluid to drain (thus preventing glaucoma) was almost 100 percent blocked in one eye and 80-90 percent blocked in the other. In the one eye there was already minimal damage indicating that she was "in trouble."

Marian was able to have surgery on each eye within a short time and should be fine from now on. The doctor thought she had probably been walking around with the condition for about a year. Marian instantly recognized God's intervention in her situation by the "assigning" of the substitute glaucoma technician to conduct her routine eye examination—but in a different and ultimately significant way.

6

SIGHTLINE

*Gazing is such a wonderful thing, about which we know little;
in gazing we are turned completely outward, but just when we are so most,
things seem to go on within us, which have been waiting longingly
for the moment when they should be unobserved.*

RAINIER MARIA RILKE

I found myself in Washington, D.C., speaking for a congress on evangelism a week after national news carried extensive coverage on race riots in a certain city of the country. Checking my departure schedule for the next morning, I discovered that my flight for home didn't leave until 11:45. "Oh, good!" I thought. "I can spend a couple hours at the National Cathedral. I can sit in the quiet and beauty of that house of prayer."

A whole morning with no responsibilities stretched before me. I could go to the Cathedral in a taxi, and from there I could catch another taxi to the airport. And since I was not planning to check baggage, I could walk right through to my gate. The phone book in my hotel room informed me of daily worship services at 7:30 a.m., a bit of a stretch after a day and night of workshops and addresses—but then I noted there was a 9:00 service in the Bethlehem Chapel. That one seemed perfect for me. How appropriate!

I'd be able to pray for the needs of our nation in the National Cathedral in the capital city.

So at eight o'clock the next morning, having enjoyed a leisurely breakfast in the Radisson, I packed my notes and clothes into my wheeled suitcase, organized my carry-on bag so that I could eventually stuff it with my purse, tucked my briefcase catty-cornered into an unzipped pocket so I could work on the flight home and checked out of the hotel. I felt quite professional, independent and competent.

Upon arriving at the Cathedral, I decided to walk through an herb garden on the grounds that I had read about once in an intriguing article. I rolled and bumped my suitcase along a stone walk, down some terraced steps and found a little corner against a stone wall to store all my baggage. Then, roaming the gardens in high heels and a business suit, I jotted notes in a notebook I rummaged from my briefcase. It was a bright May morning, crisp, with many spring flowers in full bloom. I spent a delightful thirty minutes alone in that fragrant corner, then I bumped my luggage back up the stairs, across the stone walkways and finally found the visitors entrance to the Cathedral. From that point on my morning descended rapidly downhill.

A sign informed me that the Cathedral was closed to the public until ten o'clock for cleaning. A tour group was forming, but they had pre-registered. No, a docent responded, it wouldn't be possible for me to join them. There was another open tour scheduled for eleven o'clock, she suggested—but that was too late for me. "Where is the Bethlehem Chapel?" I inquired. The guide, swishing away in a royal blue verger's gown and cap, kindly went to inquire and shortly returned to inform me that this was a service only for the Cathedral staff.

"Is there some place I can store my luggage?" I asked. At least that way I'd be able to walk the grounds unencumbered. But that too presented difficulties. I'd have to store my belongings at my own risk. And they actually preferred that I not leave them unattended since packages with bombs had been found in public buildings in Washington, D.C.

Thwarted, though in a kindly way, I departed from the visitors' entrance without so much as a glimpse at the interior of the nave. Rejected and feeling slightly miffed, I and my wheeled suitcase (piled now with my carry-on, briefcase askew and topped with my rather plump purse) bumped on the stairs and across the walks; the baggage tipped over a curb and spilled. I was surprised by the sharp pang of disappointment I felt. Somehow, through my own inadequate tourist planning (and the stuffiness of certain rules), I'd missed worship. I'd been excluded from the nave and sanctuary. I felt a little like a refugee from Chicago, not attuned to the sophisticated spiritual ways of Washington, D.C.

Suddenly I came upon a cloistered garden, with a splashing fountain, where the dogwood tree in the corner was in lush pinkish bloom and where spring sunshine sprayed the eye. Here, outside the National Cathedral, I sat on a stone bench and prayed for peace—mostly my own. It hurt not to be allowed to pray inside the Cathedral, which had a sign posted that dared to announce most publicly: This Is a House of Prayer for a People of Faith.

DULLED VISION

The most interesting aspect about the God Hunt is that we can choose to see God in our everyday circumstances or we can choose to ignore his hand. The divine has a way of pushing into our mundane disappointments if we will allow. Look, for example, at the story of Paul and Silas preaching the gospel at Philippi (Acts 16:16-34). When the two cast a spirit of divination out of a young slave girl (from whom the Philippians had been making income), they were seized by the girl's disgruntled owners. The crowd was incited against Paul and Silas, and they were attacked. The magistrates tore off their robes, beat them with rods and threw them into prison with their feet fastened in the stocks.

Amazing, Paul and Silas choose to pray and sing praises to God, and an earthquake shakes the foundations of the prison. All the doors are unlocked, and the fetters are unfastened. The two preachers, battered and abused, use this opportunity to immediately witness to the jail keeper and the other prisoners. "Believe in the Lord Jesus, and you will be saved" (Acts 16:31). What a choice these two made! In similar circumstances I would have said, "Thank God! He's rescued me!" Then I would have beaten it out of there.

Yet Paul and Silas never lost sight of their mission; they were experienced God hunters. They chose to believe that, yes, God was intervening in their world to answer their prayers; yes, he was working to extend to them unusual care, but most important, God had designed an amazing series of links and timing to help them do his work in the world. They were called to preach the gospel and preach the gospel they did.

Sitting in the cloistered garden outside the National Cathedral, I chose to wonder, *Does the Lord have anything he wants to say to me through the circumstances of this morning?* Suddenly, as though in answer, a thought of its own design intruded. *How frequently are you kept from seeing the Lord, Karen, not by other people's rules and procedures, but by the baggage you're always pulling behind you?* Perched beneath the flowering tree, reality began to push against my offended pride. I considered how often I couldn't see sanctuary because my mind was encumbered. Suitcases, notes and speeches, the right clothes and matching shoes, briefcases, purses and carry-ons!

Since I had nothing else to do at that moment, and since I was located in a beautiful place (although not exactly within the beautiful place I desired), I turned my mind to the work of self-examination. I began to pay attention to the living metaphor I had been frustratingly enacting. "Attentiveness," said Malebranche, "is the natural prayer of the soul." If all things are of God and are in God, are not all places potentially pregnant with God? "There is no place that does not see you," Ranier Maria Rilke writes at the end of his poem, "Archaic Torso of Apollo": "You must change your life."

So attend. Attend to the inner word, to the solitude made possible in this cloistered corner; to the fact that your bumbling disabilities are being observed by the One who is always seeing, and that this physical displacement is a moment laden with personal meaning. Think how uncannily your path this morning has led you to this very quiet place. Pay attention; you may have to change your life. I asked myself, *What baggage is my soul always toting?*

The answers came flooding. Too many responsibilities. The unnecessary trivia of popular culture. The pains that come from being misunderstood. Aggravations with family and colleagues. Longings for material things I can never have. And the one bit of luggage which always leaves me with purple bruises—pretensions that cause me to aspire too high. These were just a few of the concerns that dulled my vision. When I'm looking at all this stuff, I cannot be turning my eyes toward God.

I recalled the words from Matthew 17:8, "When they looked up, they saw no one except Jesus." I prayed, remembering the verse from that hymn I love so well, "Be Thou My Vision":

> Riches I heed not, nor man's empty praise,
> Thou mine Inheritance, now and always:
> Thou and Thou only, first in my heart;
> High King of heaven, my Treasure Thou art.

It would be wonderful to reach that point of spiritual maturity where I regularly lifted the eyes of my soul and saw Jesus only.

After my time of reflection I left the cloistered garden self-confessed and somewhat consoled. It's not what I had planned for the morning; I had come grandly to intercede for the state of the nation. Instead, God intervened and insisted that I humbly contend with my own spiritual state. In fact, viewing myself objectively, this whole interlude was becoming a little funny.

Bumping down more steps, my awkward pyramid of baggage toppled again. Here, a man and woman met me. I presumed they were some of the staff coming from the service in the Bethlehem Chapel. "Can we help you?" they asked. Laughing, I explained my dilemma, that I had to leave for the airport in a half-hour, that the Cathedral nave was closed for cleaning, that I had this luggage and couldn't store it anywhere, and all I wanted was to peek inside, or to even pray there.

"Oh," said the gentleman, melting me with his concern. "You're from out of town. You shouldn't be excluded from the Cathedral." He pointed out a brown door on the side of the building, back from where I'd come. "Go there," he said. "It has a handicapped access."

So I did as he said. Taking a slight risk, I stacked my baggage in a corner in the washroom, hoping anyone who came upon it would consider that its owner was appropriately occupied. Slipping through a nearby side door (here there was no cleaning announcement or a tour guide to challenge my entrance), I entered into the gorgeous interior of the Washington Cathedral. A full fifteen minutes of quiet was time enough for my disappointed soul to be uplifted with all this grace and beauty, built and dedicated to the glory of God.

Satisfied, I picked up my luggage still undisturbed and took to the path outside again, startled now by the lovely strains of a choir practice coming from some room above my head (a benediction, perhaps, to end the work of my morning). My eye followed the height of the magnificent flying buttresses, then I found myself back where I had started—at the Herb Cottage. It was ten o'clock and—after an unplanned walk around the outside of the National Cathedral, toting bag and baggage—I understood a little bit more about Christ's words, "Blessed are the pure in heart, for they shall see God."

Keeping everything on schedule with my husband's numerous conferences is not easy. Once when he was flying out of town, he needed to pick up clean shirts on his way out. He rushed to the cleaners, reaching it a few minutes after closing. However, there was someone still in the store. They hadn't locked up yet and were able to provide my husband with his clean shirts for the journey.

DEVELOPING YOUR SPIRITUAL EYE

Those of us who go on the daily God Hunt must learn to keep the object we are hunting in our sightline. God must become the fixed point of our compass. I love the moment in the film *Out of Africa* when Karen Blixen, lost on safari as she transports supplies to British officers, is met by the explorer Denys Finch Hatten. He gives her his compass and says, "Fix a place on the horizon each morning and steer by it. South by southwest. You should get there in about three days." If we are to "see" God, it will be necessary to divest ourselves of the baggage we lug behind us that preoccupies our time and attention. If we are to keep God in our sightline, we are going to have to choose a spot on the horizon each morning

and steer by it. If we want to be successful at the God Hunt, we
need to develop a trained spiritual eye. That will demand daily
practice and intentional concentration.

Most people have a dominant eye; they are either right-eyed or
left-eyed in the same way that people are either right-handed or
left-handed. In most cases, eye dominance and hand dominance
are on the same side. Some viewers are cross-dominant; that is,
their dominant hand and eye are on opposite sides. And just as
some people are ambidextrous (able to use both hands with equal
skill), some individuals do not have a dominant left or right eye, a
condition known as indeterminate eye dominance.

Even though most human beings have a dominant eye, we see
clearer when both eyes are used. Slightly different images are received from each eye; then the brain blends these disparate messages and gives us one image in addition to a sense of depth or distance. With both eyes open the viewer has a wider field of vision,
better peripheral vision and better motion detection.

In most cases, however, it is the dominant eye that aligns our
sight with the object we are viewing and helps us to sight faster.
In the case of hunters, for instance, while looking through a gun
scope (or a set of binoculars), one's field of vision can become ill-
defined. Sometimes the hunter cannot see the target as well as
with the naked eye, so he squints and adjusts the magnifications,
and by the time the field has become clear, the object he was hunting has moved beyond the sightline.

Experts in hunting strongly recommend that the hunter train
to sight from the dominant-eye side. Those who have learned to
sight by using the nondominant eye have to be retrained, and a
period of certain frustration occurs, which includes taping the
lens to strengthen the dominant eye, disciplining oneself not to
squint and waiting out the period of time before the brain can

sort out visual signals. The end result, however, is an improved skill level beyond the hunter's original abilities.

If sighting with the dominant eye is so important, how does a hunter discover which eye is dominant? What if someone has indeterminate eye dominance? What if the eyes are cross-dominant? Simple tests will quickly determine eye dominance. The first is the "coach/hunter" method. The person desiring to learn to hunt well stands several arms-lengths from the coach. They face each other squarely. Then the novice hunter places one thumb over the other and crosses the fingers of one hand over the fingers of the lower hand. This creates an ace-shaped hole, or a small triangular opening above the thumbs. The "pupil" raises his crossed hands in front of him and sights the center of the coach's nose in the opening between the fingers. The coach observes which eye is peering from the hole and whether this eye stays the same when the pupil brings his hands back to his or her face still keeping the coach's nose sighted in the opening. The hands should go to the dominant eye. This is repeated on several occasions to confirm the original results.

Another test is the finger-point method. Again, the hunter chooses a partner and a distant object. The individual points a finger at the object, keeping both eyes open and facing the object squarely. The partner covers each eye separately and alternately. When the dominant eye is covered, the finger will "jump" away from the original location.

The last test employs the use of a kaleidoscope or a paper tube of any kind. If the person is not aware of being tested for eye dominance, the tube will always be brought to the dominant eye. This also occurs with spotting scopes, telescopes or any device where single-eyed viewing is needed.

In exactly the same way, you may have to determine your spiritual eye dominance. Sit still for a while when you are disappointed in some way, excluded from the place you most desire. Run an inner eye test: ask yourself if God has had something to do with your unplanned detour. Is there a lesson he is seeking to teach you? Has he intervened in your intended progress? Conduct some rigorous self-examination: What draws your eye first? Is it the hunt for prestige, power, money, sex or fame? Be willing to retrain your vision.

On the birding trail my son says to me, "Oh, look, there is a warbler! Do you see it? In that tall tree, two to the right of the dead tree, about half-way up, on a horizontal branch with a tuft of orange leaves?" With the naked eye, I try to spot where his finger is pointing. I think I've got the tree, the branch and the fluttering bird in my sightline. But by the time I get my binoculars up and adjust their magnification, I cannot find the bird—not to mention the tree two to the right of the dead one, or the horizontal branch with a tuft of orange leaves. Everything has come so close in the magnification, it overwhelms my vision. Randall tells me this adjustment between the naked eye and the optical aid takes time and practice. Like anything else, the more I use my binoculars for sighting (and I must remember to discipline myself not to close that left eye), the better my brain will become at translating naked eye sighting to binocular sighting. I will learn to keep the object I am hunting in my sightline even as I transfer to artificial optics that eventually (I am told) will make my experience in viewing appreciably improved. The cure for indefinite sighting is just to keep looking.

How can I keep my daily vision focused on God? How can I be sure to bring my interior sight continually into play so that I can see his work in my everyday world? What can I do to guarantee that the dominant eye in my life is the spiritual eye? Why do I so often allow an indeterminate eye pattern—looking for this, searching for everything but what is of concern to my heavenly Father—to control my seeing? How can I clear the sightlines so when my eyes are lifted, I will see Jesus only? The answer to all these questions is: Just keep looking. Keep on looking.

Georgia O'Keefe, the contemporary American painter, once said, "To see takes time, like to be a friend takes time." I agree, seeing takes time—seeing God in the everyday takes practice. Yet, if I don't choose at least one moment of each day, in all the weeks and months and years of my life to ask, "Where did I see God intervene today?" won't I become an ineffectual hunter? Then who will be to blame—God? Hardly, it is the hunter who has not applied the lore of the hunt, the seeker who has not given herself to the chase.

Colossians 3:1-4 explains the training needed to make the spiritual eye the dominant eye, "Since, then, you have been raised with Christ, set your hearts on things above, where Christ is seated at the right hand of God. Set your minds on things above, not on earthly things. For you died, and your life is now hidden with Christ in God. When Christ, who is your life, appears, then you will appear with him in glory."

What intentionality this passage evokes—"set your hearts . . . set your minds . . ." Paul might also have said, Keep God and the things of God in your sightline. In order to see God's activity in our lives, we are going to have to set the optical apparatus of our souls Godward, then learn how to keep him in our scopes. We are going to have to choose to see the divine interventions in the strange interludes of living. The daily God Hunt is designed to help us do this.

THE LUMINOUS DOT

In his book *God's Human Face: The Christ-Icon,* Christoph Schoenborn examines the history of early-church theological debates over the legitimacy or illegitimacy of rendering a likeness of Christ. It is a fascinating record of the church fathers as they came to grips with the meaning and implications of the incarnation. In the book several illustrations are included in order to track the development of the art form of the human face. One is a mummy portrait reproduction from El Faiydum of Egypt. In this sample illustration a luminous dot in the eyes, representing reflected light, startles the viewer. Schoenborn asks, "Is this the first time in our history that the luminous dot is used in the eyes?" He then goes on to explain, "The slightly transparent, velvety soft, deeply glowing complexion is an expression of the living vitality of the deceased, in the same way as also the large, shining eyes, which seem to be filled with the splendor of eternal life they now behold."

Oh God, as I choose to seek for you in the every day, let a luminous dot glow in my eye. Help my slight human sight catch, even now, splintered glimpses of the eternal splendor. Give me, I pray, a dominant spiritual eye. Make the eyes of my soul lidless.

Be Thou my vision, O Lord of my heart;
Naught be all else to me, save that Thou art.
Thou my best thought, by day or by night,
Waking or sleeping, thy presence my light.

Sighting

Gail MacDonald writes about meetings she and her husband, Gordon, conducted overseas. The response of the couples being taught under the circumstances and the freedom to teach are all indicators of God's help to do his work in the world.

Our time in Germany was equally amazing. We came away so heartened by the power of God's Spirit to come and open hearts, bring couples together and change us all. Speaking through a translator is challenging, but we quickly got our rhythm and made it a fun time too. At the end we were shocked when they told us that 97% of the 70 couples who came bought all five tapes. Who would buy tapes where you are speaking through a translator?

This was a sign to us that God came and will continue the work he began there. Gordon and I had such a tenderness with each other, and things we hadn't planned on saying just flowed between us back and forth like a lovely dance.

7

HUNTING GEAR AND
MASTER HUNTERS

*But the word is very near you; it is in your mouth
and in your heart, so that you can do it*

DEUTERONOMY 30:14 RSV

David and I fell into conversation at the dinner table with the
Salvation Army officers we were getting to know at a Cascade Di-
visional Officers' retreat at the Timberline Lodge on Mount
Hood above Portland, Oregon. "What kind of recreational activities do you enjoy?" we asked one husband and wife. They loved
to bicycle and they loved to hike. "Ever been lost?" I wondered.
Yes, they'd lost their way once or twice, but nothing so serious that
someone had to call out the Forest Rangers.

Then the wife, Susan, went on to volunteer that on mountain-
sides, such as where we were now, above the treeline there weren't
the normal sort of trail markers you might find in a more verdant
terrain—blazes on trees, directional signage or a wooded trail that
leads onward. Here, there were only rocks. In mountains like this,
or in the desert, the openness tends to make everything look like
a trail! In addition, crisscrossing footpaths left by hikers and the
stamping of cattle on delicate desert plants can lead to a confusing
network of paths. "What they do in areas like this is stack stones,"

Susan explained. "They're called ducks. At least three stacked stones, sometimes more, along the path and always within your line of vision. If they fall down, you stack them again for those coming on the path behind you. You sight by these stones; they help you to find your way."

As we embark on the daily God hunt we need to stack stones as well—stones that will keep us moving along the trail and prevent us from veering away. What are these stones? Scripture, prayer, meditation, godly people. Used wisely, these stones can keep us from getting lost or confused.

We had agreed to provide free training for a division of Salvation Army officers in the Mainstay Communication Model (a preparation method that is designed to enhance life-changing response on the part of the hearer) if we could also present the way the Model is integrated into our spiritual growth tools. We enjoyed the exchange with these folk enormously, and two weeks after we returned home, we also received an unexpected check for $500. Since this was during a "late-paycheck" season, the gift helped us enormously.

SCRIPTURAL STONES

One significant work that has radicalized my approach to reading Scripture is the book *The Word Is Very Near You: A Guide to Praying with Scripture* by Martin L. Smith. It is a rich, soulful read accompanied by practical Scripture/prayer exercises. Smith writes, "In recent decades many Christians have been coming to the painful recognition that our spirituality has been deeply infected for a long time by the same alienations that wrack our society, and that defects and distortions in Christian teaching going back for centuries have actually contributed to our estrangement." One of the estrangements he seeks to heal is the way we use Scripture.

First, we must understand that to meditate on the Word means that we should chew on the Scriptures in the same way that cows vigorously and rhythmically chew their cud! "How sweet are your words to my taste, sweeter than honey to my mouth! . . . I open my mouth and pant, longing for your commands" (Psalm 119:103, 131). We want to mull the taste of the words and their meanings over and over.

Often Christians eat the right spiritual food, but consume it in the wrong way. For some, there is a tendency to stuff themselves. The body can only absorb so many nutritional supplements before sloughing them off as waste. Similarly, Robert Mulholland Jr. of Asbury Seminary in Wilmore, Kentucky, makes a powerful point about spiritual feeding in his book *Shaped by the Word*. He distinguishes between approaching the Word of God for information or for transformation. The following contrast can have convicting implications:

Informational reading of Scripture

- seeks to cover as much as possible as quickly as possible

- is linear and demonstrates the thinking that reading is little more than covering all the parts

- seeks to master the texts

- considers that the texts exist for us to control or manipulate according to our interests and desires

- is analytical, critical and judgmental

- is characterized by a problem-solving mentality

Transformational reading of Scripture

- seeks to meet with God, taking as much time as needed to pour over the texts until they get through the reader

- is in-depth reading

- seeks to allow the text to master us

- allows oneself to be controlled and conformed by the reading

- requires a humble, detached, receptive, loving approach

- holds an openness to mystery, to the mystery we call God

Some of us are hungry because we aren't feeding on the Word in the right way.

David, my husband, often has to remind me at mealtimes, "Slow down. Enjoy what you're eating. Don't eat so fast." Are you eating the Word too fast, for information only? Is this one reason your soul feels famished, unsatisfied, without nourishment? Don't just grab a morsel, stuff it into your mouth and then hurry on. Slow down. Taste your food. Chew before swallowing. Savor your meal. We know we have taken in Scripture the right way when we feel satisfied and have as much as we want, when we come away thinking about what needs to be changed in our attitude or absorbed into our living.

Benedict, the founder of the Benedictine order, felt it was a sin to go to Scripture for intellectual information only. Esther de Waal, who has developed a contemporary commentary on his monastic rule in her book *Seeking for God: The Way of St. Benedict,* writes that according to Benedict, "So the Scriptures are mouthed by the lips, understood by the intelligence, fixed by the memory, and finally the will comes into play and what has been read is also put into practice. The act of reading makes the reader become a different person; reading cannot be separated from living."

Martin Smith explains, "Meditation on the Scriptures was so much the basis of monastic spirituality in the church that this experience . . . gave rise to a scheme of biblical interpretation which guided prayer for over a thousand years." The scheme included four deepening ways of interpreting the biblical stories and passages that have, until recently, almost been forgotten outside monasteries. The four levels begin with

> the literal sense in which we deal with the manifest, historical meaning of the text. The second approach is through the allegorical sense in which the text symbolically points to the person and work of Christ. The third approach is through the moral sense in which we let the text summon us to repent and change the way we live. The fourth approach is through the anagogical sense in which the text elicits from us in contemplation our transcendent desire to be united with God.

This approach is a far cry from the "quiet time" tradition in which Christians are instructed to take ten or twenty minutes each morning to read their Bible and pray. What we are looking for is a transformational model.

I am stacking ducks along my daily path, scriptural stones that help me as I go on the God Hunt to keep the object I am hunting within my spiritual sightlines. They are signs along my path named Every Day. They remind me as I am moving forward that what I am looking for is God's work. He is active so I must stay awake. Martin Smith writes:

> Israel's God was all initiative. The living God acted and spoke first, choosing, wooing, calling, inviting. Experience

was marked all over with the print of otherness, encounter with unpredictable, uncalled-for, surprising, endlessly versatile action and manifestation. Religion is supremely responsive. The whole of existence, the individual's and the community's, is a conversation which God begins. In prayer, as in life, we are the ones who answer. God touches us, God speaks to us, God moves us, God reveals truth to us, and life and prayer is our response.

MASTER HUNTERS AND PRAYER

Master hunters are those rare men or women who seem so alive to God that your desire to play the game of hide-and-seek is deepened, quickened by them. They have a lore of spirituality, practiced knowledge to share, and yet they are particularly at ease in not needing to "fix" you, realizing that this is the role of the Holy Spirit. Master hunters can be holy people from the past whose words and experiences with God speak to us from the centuries or from the decades, or people from our lives who teach us from their own wisdom and experience. We may have trouble finding living, human master hunters, but there is no excuse for not putting ourselves into a learning posture with those who are already dead.

My Covenant Group has been meeting together monthly for over a decade. These women, who are all involved in full-time Christian ministry, are some of the master hunters I have put into my life to teach me the lore of the trail and to keep me on the path. I have benefited deeply from the teaching gifts of each of my dear friends.

Recently one of the women, Marilyn Stewart, who with her husband, Doug, is in charge of spiritual formation for the senior staff at InterVarsity Christian Fellowship, was showing us how she uses Scripture throughout the day to consciously turn her heart toward God. She recommended *The Divine Hours,* a book of readings compiled by Phyllis Tickle that draws on the Anglican Book of Common Prayer with chosen readings from the church fathers and modernizes the ancient concept of fixed-hour prayer. The hours recognized in Phyllis Tickle's book are four:

- the morning office (to be observed on the hour or half hour between 6 and 9 a.m.)

- the midday office (to be observed on the hour or half hour between 11 a.m. and 2 p.m.)

- the vespers office (to be observed on the hour or half hour between 5 and 8 p.m.)

- the night office (to be observed before retiring)

This is a useful format for devotion, already created, for any busy individual wishing for a way to build a practice of spiritual regularity into the day. The readings each take only a few minutes, focus the mind, remind us of whom it is we are really seeking and can be shared corporately with family members, friends or Christian coworkers. They are stacked stones that mark the path.

Fixed hours of prayer were originally practiced by the Israelites of the Old Testament. They observed a daily morning and evening sacrifice, and prayed at the three appointed times during the third, sixth and ninth hours. The practice of praying at fixed hours was continued in New Testament times. In Acts 10:9 we read that Peter went up on the housetop to pray at "about the sixth hour" (RSV), and in Acts 3:1 Peter and John went up into the temple at "the hour of prayer, the ninth hour" (RSV).

After the sixth century, and due to the influence of Benedict, the prescribed hours were standardized at seven. Distinct prayers were specified for these times: matins and nocturns at midnight; lauds, following immediately after; prime at sunrise; terce at midmorning; sext at noon; nones at midafternoon; vespers and evening prayer at eventide; and compline at bedtime. In Benedictine communities today, five to seven offices of prayer are observed, depending on the unique "customary" of the house. The bell rings, calling the community to services, and in many places, even in the middle of the night, men and women rise to perform the works of communal devotion.

In *The Cloister Walk,* Kathleen Norris writes:

Few books have so strongly influenced Western history as *The Rule of St. Benedict.* Written in the sixth century, a time as violent and troubled as our own, by a man determined to find a life of peace and stability for himself and others, it is a brief (ninety-six pages in a recent English translation), practical, and thoughtful work on how humans beings can best live in community. Its style is so succinct that it is sometimes taught in law schools as an example of how to legislate simply and well. But the true power of the book, as with the Gospel it is based on, lies in its power to change lives.

Ah, here we have one of those dead master hunters with rich counsel to share for our trek through our days. Attend! Attend!

My goal is to keep my mind continually drawing toward finding the presence of my Creator in each moment. In order to do this I must (at a minimum)

- observe evening prayers
- quote Scripture in the middle of the night if I wake before day
- observe morning prayers

- read a Psalm at noon (a Benedictine community recites or sings psalms at morning, noon and evening prayer, going through the Psalter every three to four weeks)

- say evening prayers again

Believe me, this takes effort, but I try never to let a pile of stacked stones get out of my line of vision.

At the end of a particularly discouraging day, during a hard and difficult season in our lives, the words of the readings for evening prayers said over and over to me, "Don't be discouraged."

From the Psalms: "Restore our fortunes, O LORD, like the watercourses of the Negev."

From the Hymn: "The King of love my shepherd is, whose goodness fails me never / In death's dark vale I fear no ill, with you, dear Lord, beside me / And so through all the length of days, your goodness fails me never."

From the Refrain: "Those who sowed with tears will reap with songs of joy."

It was hard not to get God's point for that evening.

The next suggestion made by my friend was to use the Lord's Prayer as a repeated litany throughout the day. "Read the phrases slowly—slowly," Marilyn insisted, and made sure we did so, out loud, twice. This practice has been having great effect for me. Generally when I wake, my mind rushes to action; there is no slow winding up to get into the day for me. Now, however, when I wake, I slowly, slowly repeat each phrase of the Lord's Prayer:

> Our father which art in heaven, hallowed be thy name.
> Thy kingdom come. Thy will be done, on earth,
>   as it is in heaven.
> Give us this day our daily bread.
> And forgive us our debts, as we forgive our debtors.
> And lead us not into temptation, but deliver us from evil:
> For thine is the kingdom, and the power, and the glory,
>   for ever, Amen.

If I finish, I repeat the passage. (For some reason, I rarely reach *Give us this day our daily bread* before falling back to sleep again; there must be a soporific effect in the intonation.) Amazing, this prayer points my slumbering self toward God and keeps all the responsibilities and duties and ministry concerns and daily plans from rushing in and bullying my consciousness.

I also try to fall into sleep praying the Lord's Prayer or repeating one of the many passages from Scripture I am memorizing. Right now I am learning the cadences from Colossians 1, "He is the image of the invisible God, the first-born of all creation; for in him all things were created, in heaven and on earth" (RSV). This practice immediately wards off all those nagging responsibilities that habitually waylay me. Some people set their alarms before they go to bed so they will not oversleep in the morning; I am setting my heart to God so I will not forget to hunt for him.

Prayer doesn't have to occur only at fixed times though. We can be seeking God through prayer at any hour of the day. The ancient prayers of the Celtic Christian communities demonstrate an understanding of the potential sanctity of every moment. There are prayers for waking, prayers for dressing, prayers for going out and coming in. There are prayers that consecrate the seed planted in the earth, prayers for reaping, prayers for driving the cows, for milking and for clipping sheep. There are blessings for house-holds, for meals and for "smooring" the fire on the hearth. There's an invocation at churning and for warping; there are nighttime blessings, prayers for worship and adoration, prayers for dying. One of those prayers goes like this:

> May God free me from every wickedness,
> May God free me from every entrapment,
> May God free me from every gully, from every tortuous road,
>   from every slough.
> May God open to me every pass,
> Christ open to me every narrow way,
> Each soul of holy man and woman in heaven
> Be preparing me for my pathway.

These prayers were the "stones" these people placed beside the paths of their days so they would not forget God, to whom they owed life and their place in the world.

A PERSONAL LITURGY

The third practice Marilyn suggested was to write a personal lit-urgy that would not take more than a few minutes to repeat. Most often we think of liturgy in terms of corporate worship or prayer services, but a liturgy can also be personal, helping us enter into worship, to become present to God. Many Christians, not raised in liturgical churches, have discovered that liturgy can allow them to enter into prayers and Scriptures in a way that is not strictly ra-tional, and can restore a connection between the head's way of knowing and the heart's way of understanding.

Marilyn uses this tool upon waking in the morning, before go-ing to sleep at night, when she is afraid or aware of failure, and when she is attempting to still herself before God. Over time this personal formula allows the Word of God to seep into our souls.

Marilyn provided an outline to help in preparation. It includes

- an introduction, or a preamble, to prepare your heart to meet God.

- an Old Testament text that has special meaning; one that helps you remember a trait or characteristic of God that you have difficulty believing. This is a verse that in some way touches the heart.

- the words of a hymn, preferably one that uses a "we" theme, which gives a sense of the larger body of Christ.

- a New Testament text that has spoken to you.

- a one or two sentence prayer, which is a cry of your heart and which focuses you to the point where God is speaking.

- a word from the writings of the men and women of the church, to move you from your own context to that of the larger body over the centuries.

- an epilogue or closing word of some kind that brings the whole personal liturgy together.

I have taken Marilyn's advice and have written a personal liturgy and am beginning to memorize the words. I begin these memorized prayers and readings by taking a moment to think, *How is it I have seen God today?* Here's my liturgy to give you an idea of what it might look like.

THE INTRODUCTORY PRAYER

God, I thank you that I have seen you intervening in my life in this way _____*(name some sighting that has occurred today).*

Grant me, O Lord my God,
a mind to know you,
a heart to seek you,
wisdom to find you,
conduct pleasing to you,
faithful perseverance in waiting for you,
and a hope of finally embracing you.

THOMAS AQUINAS

OLD TESTAMENT TEXT

Oh come, let us sing to the LORD ;
let us make a joyful noise to the rock of our salvation!
Let us come into his presence with thanksgiving;
let us make a joyful noise to him with songs of praise!
For the LORD is a great God,
and a great King above all gods.
In his hand are the depths of the earth;
the heights of the mountains are his also.
The sea is his, for he made it;
for his hands formed the dry land.
O come, let us worship and bow down,
let us kneel before the LORD, our Maker!
For he is our God,
and we are the people of his pasture,

PSALM 95:1-7 RSV

HYMN OF THE CHURCH

O, the deep, deep love of Jesus, vast, unmeasured, boundless, free!
Rolling as a mighty ocean in its fullness over me!
Underneath me, all around me, is the current of His love;
Leading onward, leading homeward, to my glorious rest above.
O, the deep, deep love of Jesus, love of every love the best;

'Tis an ocean vast of blessing, 'tis the source of peace and rest.
O, the deep, deep love of Jesus, 'tis a heav'n of heav'ns to me;
And it lifts me up to glory, for it lifts me up to Thee.
O, the deep, deep love of Jesus, spread his praise from shore to shore;
Sing of His greatness, sing of His goodness, sing of His love forevermore.

SAMUEL TREVOR FRANCIS/ THOMAS J. WILLIAMS,
"O THE DEEP, DEEP LOVE OF JESUS"

NEW TESTAMENT TEXT

That which was from the beginning, which we have heard, which we have seen with our eyes, which we have looked upon and touched with our hands, concerning the world of life—the life was made manifest, and we saw it, and testify to it, and proclaim to you the eternal life which was with the Father and was made manifest to us—that which we have seen and heard we proclaim also to you, so that you may have fellowship with us; and our fellowship is with the father and with his Son Jesus Christ.

1 JOHN 1:1-3 RSV

PRAYER

Heavenly Father, in you we live and move and have our being: We humbly pray to you so to guide and govern us by your Holy Spirit, that in all the cares and occupations of our life we may not forget you, but may remember that we are ever walking in your sight; through Jesus Christ our Lord. Amen.

WORD OF THE CHURCH

We believe in one God,
the Father, the Almighty,
maker of heaven and earth,
of all that is, seen and unseen.
We believe in one Lord, Jesus Christ,
the only Son of God,

eternally begotten of the Father,
God from God, Light from Light,
true God from true God,
begotten, not made,
of one Being with the Father.
We believe in the Holy Spirit, the Lord, the giver of life,
who proceeds from the Father and the Son.
With the Father and the Son he is worshiped and glorified.

AN EXCERPT FROM THE NICENE CREED

EPILOGUE

So dare to be as once he was who came to live, and love, and die.

GAUDEAMUS DOMINO

The gifts of my friend Marilyn Stewart, a master hunter, when practiced keep me turning my face toward God. "Here's looking at you," a well-known line spoken by Humphrey Bogart, is my word to God throughout the day. The eyes of my soul are cast his way. These are stones stacked along my path.

Most of us live secular lives, with a Christian moment intruding here and there. The days unfold before us, their hours piling one upon the other, crowding our sleep, taking our thoughts and actions hostage. Hardly, rarely, only intermittently do we think of God.

We should instead be diligent about building a Christian life, with secular moments intruding here and there. I don't want to fall exhausted into sleep before I stack at least three stones to guard my nighttime hours. I don't want my rest interrupted at night without first turning my mind to God. I don't want to rush into the day collecting the tasks and duties in a suitcase as I bang out the door. No, I want to put these stacked stones—

praying Scripture throughout the day, observing fixed hours of prayer and Scripture reading, designing a personal liturgy—just within my vision, to remind me that I need to keep God always in my sightline.

What stones are you stacking beside your daily path?

$\mathcal{S}ighting$

Marian Oliver experienced a profound intervention in the timing of her father's death. Living in Maryland, he called on a Saturday to tell her that he was having side effects from the radiation therapy for prostate cancer. "If ever I needed you to come, now's the time." Though she was scheduled to attend a pastor's retreat at Mainstay Ministries, she was able to fly out to her parents' home on Monday, using free passes from a friend who was a United Airlines employee. About five hours after she arrived home, Marian's father suddenly died.

She says, "I saw God at work in moving my heart to go (I had been sick) and in allowing me to get there before he died, because if Mom had had to face this situation alone with her advanced Alzheimer's, I can't even imagine what she would have done or how the situation would have been handled. I just can't imagine."

8

KEEPING A LIFE LIST

From the Song of Songs to Jubilate Agno and "Song of Myself,"
the catalog has been used as a form of praise.

EDWARD HIRSCH

Insomnia has been a good friend—I owe my prayer life to it. Those long nights years ago when David and I were in the pastorate —worrying about the church's dissident faction. Those limping minutes before morning when the grief of a broken life or the co-malike sleep of my exhausted husband gnawed holes in my soul— oh, if day would just come! Nighttime pain has no balm, none of the distractions that fill wakeful hours. And the nights of church board meetings—well, forget it, sleep was a recalcitrant child, howling and fighting against bedtime. It wasn't just pain that kept me awake; joy could chase away slumber as well—the laughter and caffeine of a dinner party, spiritual nativity occurring right in our living room, or good conversation that shot off my mental chemicals in bright inward bursts of fireworks.

After a while I decided that I might as well put the restless nights to useful employment. I began spraying cleaner on charcoal ovens at 1:30 a.m., pushing laundry and tearing apart messy closets. Whereas this was progress in terms of household organization, some of the seminarians who lived with us in those years often muttered comments through clenched teeth, such as,

"What on earth were you doing last night at three o'clock?" So I scratched the time-efficient, management-effective plan and took up the discipline of prayer during my times of sleeplessness. It was quiet and came highly recommended (and had up to this point been boring); maybe it would put me back to sleep.

While insomnia became the friend that turned me toward prayer, what truly transformed me into a pray-before-you-do-anything-else woman was the habit of keeping a prayer journal. Each day's entry in my thirty-some spiral notebooks begins with a record of how I have sighted God in my everyday world (that is quite a body of evidence!). In over thirty years of keeping a journal, I have never had a day in which I have not had something to write in the God Hunt section. Without a doubt, of all the devotional disciplines in my life, the journaling of my prayers is one that has most prodded my spiritual growth.

One July day I wrote in my prayer journal, "We are languishing here in Egypt. There are no roads forward." That day I received a poem from a friend and I pasted it on the next page of my journal. The last stanza reads, "When I consider how you consented to enclosure/in Mary's womb/in a narrow manger/in a carpenter's home/on the wooden cross/my heart is moved to seek enclosure with you. Amen."

Why is this? First of all, journaling my prayers makes my spiritual life concrete, firm, knowable. I can see where I have been, where I have struggled and how far I have come by the simple recording of my daily prayers. Because I jot down answered prayers in the columns of the notebooks I use, I know what I have prayed about and how God has responded. As prayer journals should be, mine has been an ongoing portrait on paper of a soul bare before God; I have captured times when I've been spiritually hungry or disappointed or elated or distressed.

In fact, without knowing it, years ago when I began journaling my prayers, I actually began a life list (such as birders keep to record all the species they identify in a lifetime), capturing on paper all the God Hunt sightings I have identified through the days of my life. By their sheer numbers these profound evidences overwhelmingly prove to me that life is full of often unrecognized encounters with the divine. My life list shows me, helps me to remember, and sometimes convinces me again that God is always, everywhere, all the time, day and night, intervening on my behalf. When I choose to recognize his activity and write it down, I am keeping spiritual field notes that have informed my living, my writing, my thinking and my being now for over thirty years.

The journals not only make the journey of the soul concrete for me; they are also proof of spiritual life to those who don't know where to begin or how to get started. Often when I'm speaking to young people on spiritual growth, I'll drag out a box of my prayer journals, pile the notebooks on a table and say, "I'm going to talk to you about prayer. This is what five years of prayer look like." Suddenly the attitude in the room changes from "What could this woman possibly have to say to me?" to "Oh, she's going to talk about prayer! She must know something about the topic; there's the evidence in that pile of journals on the table."

The beauty of a prayer journal is that it doesn't have to look like the journal of anyone else. David, my husband, is a super-organized man who goes to his prayer notes three times a day. He folds an $8\frac{1}{2}$-by-11-inch piece of lined paper into fourths, snaps it into his three-ring folder, labels each column with headers (such as "Thanksgiving") and then makes lists of words under each header. (It is amazing how much can be conveyed by one or two appropriate word reminders!) Then his prayer journal is divided into sections; the three-ring binder allows him to change the pages around. He marks his place in the intercession section by moving a paper clip down the lines to indicate to himself that he has prayed for these items and can move onto the next.

DAVID'S LIST

- Answers to prayer about next Adventure
- Found Christmas store and had time between conferences to buy ornaments for family
- Know who driver was who knocked down power lines
- Store buys Advent calendars from Randall
- Extra time so I can visit Becky's hospital
- Delay on Advent—superheroes—gives time
- Good conversation with Mary on resurrection
- Karen's chapters fit next series and are great
- How quickly learning took place at conference I taught
- A debt canceled
- Jeff—perfect contact for Advent work
- John fills in for Karen
- Name change on Advent from Jerry is good
- Cleaner—got there one minute before closing; someone still in store
- Jenae's help at Detroit conference
- Good sales despite materials going to wrong church
- Time with grandchildren—great diversion

- Got to see Veggie Xmas video at last minute
- Philippian jailer illustration for Karen
- Yes on IV video—answer to prayer
- Remortgaging goes through
- Found glasses case
- Met Jeremy's new girlfriend by chance
- Alan's qualifications what we need
- Karen travels and helps with driving
- Flight not crowded
- Mark's piece for Advent calendar works
- Ross helps in San Jose and is great
- Tammy calls on Fairfield Inn lady

I too have a system of categories I pray through each day, beginning with the God Hunt, but my list beneath each topic takes more space since I express myself in phrases, sentences and sometimes paragraphs. Despite the differences, the prayer journal prods both David and me to focus on our spiritual life and to record the ongoing work of God in our everyday experience. Stacks of journals remind me of God's love for me over the year. At any time I can look back and remember the ways he has intervened in my daily life—obvious answers to my prayers, extended to me and the ones I love; unexpected evidences of his care; generous help to do God's work in the world; and many, many incidents of unusual linkage and timing. Reviewing any of the journals reminds me of what I have come to know about my Maker—I see evidences of his mercy, his humor, his loving tolerance, his patient forgiveness, and sometimes, his penchant for silence.

KAREN'S LIST

January 15, 2003

I saw you God yesterday—

- A good sales day—$27,000 in conferences and phones
- British Air charge finally off card; fax to travel agent
- David recovering quickly from bad cold
- Randall already taking Atlanta conference so David didn't have to travel
- A lovely girlfriend for Jeremy
- Titles and artwork and product list almost done
- Final appeal for February almost together
- Three pilgrims to Spain canceled; three more considering—still full
- Protection for Laurie and Elias in traffic hazard
- Laughing time after a long fourteen-hour work day with grandchildren—so adorable and so relaxing
- Spiritual disciplines at work in all this
- The gift of prayer; hours spent in praise and intercession

YOUR PRAYER JOURNAL

Keeping a record of God's daily work over a lifetime is a powerful way to know him. Have you tried journaling before and failed? Why not try again? Experiment with a different format this time. Ask yourself the question, *What kind of journal works best for me?* If for a while you don't keep up with this discipline, pick up your neglected prayer journal without self-chastisement and begin again. Nudging any kind of an exercise toward discipline always includes stops and starts.

Be assured that the whys and hows of journaling are up to the diarist. Some people work better in their journals in the morning. I am an early morning person, and I love to start my day ordering my soul before the Lord, examining yesterday's evidence of God. My husband, on the other hand, is a night person, so before he prepares for bed, he looks back over his day and records the work of God in his journal. No matter whether you thrive in the morning, midday or night, you must find the formula that is personal for you. In the book *English Diaries,* editor Arthur Posonby verifies this individuality: "Diarists need only consult their own convenience and mood, they need obey no rules, they may follow their own inclination to write regularly, irregularly, fully or briefly."

You don't have to be a literary giant to keep a good journal. In an article on the topic, *Psychology Today* noted, "Last year, thousands of Americans with no literary pretensions whatsoever started producing stories of surpassing interest that will probably never be published. They were writing their own, often eye-popping, tear-evoking journals, not because they felt they needed therapy, but because they wanted to put their lives into perspective and find in them some deeper meaning."

In fact, it is important not to give into the pretensions that urge us to leave behind a record that is publishable. An acquaintance I once knew explained that she had sworn a friend to promise to burn all her journals should anything tragic happen. "I couldn't write freely if I thought someone would be reading what I wrote after I died," she explained.

An imperative rule to follow when writing a prayer journal is to avoid editing. Your writing does not have to be grammatically correct (or politically correct); what you are trying to capture are those instant impressions of your soul in a state of being awakened to your God. You need to be free to be frank, honest with your emotions and self-revealing.

Look at this enchanting entry from the diary of Elizabeth Fry, the one-day Quaker prison reformer, "I went to town feeling very close to God, but being seen and admired by some officers sent me home as filled with the world as I went to town filled with Heaven." She was sixteen. Later on as an adult she wrote again about keeping records, "That is the advantage of a true journal. It leads the mind to look inwards."

Journaling puts us in the company of the great heroes of faith. John Wesley, for example, kept a diary for sixty-six years. His journal has been called "the most amazing record of human exertion ever penned or endured." In his diary Wesley attributed the secret of his immense physical strength to "the good pleasure of God," which enabled him to "constantly rise at four for about fifty years; generally preach at five in the mornings, one of the most healthy exercises in the world; and never travel less, by sea or land, than four thousand five hundred miles in a year."

Dr. John Rutty's spiritual diary, written in the 1700s, includes these comments: "I have been putting the cart (i.e. the body) before the horse (i.e. the soul) all my life: But God is turning me around. . . . O, what a trial is prosperity! The reins must be held tighter in time of plenty. Spent my matin in spiritual fox hunting. . . . The afternoon meeting was partly silent, partly loquacious; the silent part was more edifying than the preaching; what a pity it is that some persons know not when to leave off!"

SPIRITUAL POVERTY AND GROWTH

In an experimental program, three hundred recruits from a city's welfare and unemployment rolls were taught journal-keeping skills as part of their on-the-job training as nurses' aides, security guards, maintenance personnel, housekeepers and dietary workers. Ninety percent of the recruits kept their journals over a six-month period, finished their training and stayed on to perform their low-status positions. After a year 80 percent were still employed or had taken better jobs. One in three had moved into improved housing; one in four had actually started night school or community college.

Would you believe that much of the credit for this advancement was given to the journal-keeping discipline? The director of the experiment stated, "Poverty is not simply the lack of money. Ultimately, it is a person's lack of feeling for the reality of one's own inner being."

Spiritual poverty could be defined in much the same terms. The spiritually impoverished believer has a lack of feeling for the reality of his or her own inner being and the relationship of that being to God. Maybe you're someone who feels like you live a low-stakes spiritual existence. It's not that you haven't tried, but for too long your relationship with the Lord has been at a standstill. The time-honored practice of keeping a spiritual prayer journal stimulates journal-keepers to experience accelerated, measurable and long-term spiritual growth.

The committed diarist will advance out of the pablum, spoon-feeding necessary for young immature Christians into taking responsibility for one's own spiritual state and the growth needed for it to progress.

George F. Simon writes in *Keeping Your Own Personal Journal,* "The journal is a place where tender new growth is privately and secretly nourished, away from the burning eyes and the blasting voices of others. It is the hidden chamber where awkward new steps can be practiced until we are sure enough to take them out into everyday life. A journal is . . . an ongoing book, which will be a continuing response to the nagging question 'Who am I?'"

A journal gives its owner a concrete means of evaluating personal spiritual growth. Re-reading and reviewing a prayer journal is important. We see where and what we have been, how far we have come and where it is we must go. Because a journal can be reviewed from time to time, it also has a stabilizing influence. The long view of our personal development keeps us from the temptation of becoming overwhelmed by our present failures or from becoming discouraged by today's painful circumstances.

In discouraging months this printed Scripture came to me, mailed by one of our donors. It is pasted as a reminder in my prayer journal after several pages of complaints that God was not doing what I needed him to do. "And David said to Solomon his son, 'Be strong and of good courage, and do it: fear not, nor be dismayed: for the LORD God, even my God, will be with thee; he will not fail thee, nor forsake thee, until thou hast finished all the work for the service of the house of the LORD.'"
(1 Chronicles 28:20 KJV)

One man who kept a journal for many years made a point of re-reading the corresponding entries from previous years on the same date on which he was writing his present journal. A friend of mine takes a few days at the end or beginning of the New Year to reassess the lessons and themes of the old year. She has organized her approach to this into categories, writes conclusions, then uses this synopsis as a point of referral as she moves on into the new season of her life.

Most important, a spiritual diary encourages our awareness of our unique place before God and our unique journey with him. In fact, there is no better tool with which I am familiar that develops our capacity for spiritual sightings. Did you ask something of God? Did you make a request? Did God grant you favor? How do you remember this? Write it down. Record both your request and the way in which it was answered. In what ways has God preserved your life? Keep a life list, all the records of divine activity in one place. How has he given you significance in ministry? How has he chosen to use you? Write it down. Write it down.

IMMENSE INTIMACY, INTIMATE IMMENSITY

One fall when my oldest son was still in college, he and I stole a day away together. We headed toward a wildlife sanctuary in Wisconsin where Canada geese water on their migratory flights. Since the migratory activity was quiet on this day, Randall and I took to the trails and attempted to make other bird sightings. The dun-colored underbrush and the fallen leaves on the path created a world that was darkly monochromatic, not shot through with brilliant fall oranges and golds, or with extroverted reds; we were slipping into that season, a wintering world, when the beauty is in the browns. "Shhhh," my son whispered, tugging on my arm to stop me. "Deer. In the bush. To your left." I looked, swept my eyes, squinted, but saw nothing. "Where?" I whispered. He made a small motion, pointing, "About fifteen feet in front of you."

Sure enough, still-standing and barely beyond reach was a dusky female doe, her large round eyes staring blackly at us; her muscles tensed to bound away should we make any motion toward her. Without Randall's keen vision, his highly developed hunting eye, I would have plodded along, kicking the leaves in front of me, scanning for fluttering motion, wing-beats on the bushes, and totally bypassed the exquisite creature whose hide blended gently into the brown-brushed world around us. We stared at each other for a long moment, the human creatures observing and being observed by the animal creature. Then with a flick of motion, she disappeared from sight.

Keeping a life list helps us to see God, to see the obvious activity right in front of our eyes. It is as simple as that. When I go back over the weeks of my prayer journal, I make notations as to which prayers have been answered, and I remember where I have been and what God has been doing with me. Every once in a while I grab a handful of notebooks and recall his work over a series of years. The journals have informed my writing, reminded me of details that would have slipped far beyond my recall. But mostly they have developed in me the habit of seeing. My capacity for in-attention, my great sin of lapsed spiritual attention, is continually adjusted into focus when I ask myself the question each day of my life, "Where is it that I saw God today?"

The discipline of writing down my sightings (and having done so for over thirty years) is not unlike a serious birdwatcher's practice of recording a list of bird sightings. A life list posted by "Birding World" is nineteen pages long and includes a total number of 488 sightings as of a certain date. Listen to the lovely poetry in some of these names

- Great Northern Diver Gavia immer

- Fulmar Fulmarus glacialis glacialis

- Balearic Shearwater Puffinus mauretanicus

- Storm Petral Hydrobates pealgicus

- Ruddy Shelduck Tadorna ferruginea

- Red-breasted Merganser Mergus serrator

For me, a wordsmith, it would be worth keeping a birding life list just to have this amazing phonic liturgy to intone, to wind my tongue and mouth around the syllables, the feathered poetics of unintentional spondees, trochees, parallelisms (glacialis glacialis) and vers libre. This is flight language, born on the soul of those who love to observe the winged waywardness of skyborne things.

Some birders compile a life list for the United States, some for the world, and some for their back yard. My son Randall keeps a list with a goal to sight 244 birds by the end of December.

An "elite" birder might set a life goal of sighting a certain number of the eight to nine thousand birds possible to be identified worldwide. This would mean the investment of unlimited time, money for travel, and resolve, but Randall reminds me that the thrill is heightened by spying a bird you have never seen before.

The same thrill comes from sighting God, and the practice of keeping a life list makes us apt in observing God's ways in our days. I love the sighting story Tim Jones has included in an article about writer and Presbyterian minister Frederick Buechner. Buechner was parked in his car by a Vermont road not far from his home, anxious about the anorexic condition of his teenage daughter, when along whizzed another car bearing the license plate with the word TRUST. Buechner states, "Of all the entries in the lexicon of words that I needed most to hear, it was that word *trust*. It was a chance thing, but also a moment of epiphany— revelation—telling me, 'Trust your children, trust yourself, trust God, trust life; just *trust*.'"

Those who have eyes to see, who have made a deliberate effort to cultivate a hunter's expertise, who like the writer Buechner have recorded the works of God in some personal way, then pondered them, will discover the sacred message in the chance encounters, and learn that nothing, nothing happens to us that is outside his divine providence. Eventually that license plate made its way to the writer's wall when the trust officer of a local bank delivered it to Buechner's hands, having heard about this illustration used in sermons. (Obviously the word *trust* held totally different contexts for the two men.)

Keeping a life list of God Hunt sightings helps us to see with the eyes of our soul the God who calls us to the game of hide-and-go-seek and always meets us in the chase. Hunters who journal their sightings for a lifetime will grow replete in their souls. Christ said, "Blessed are your eyes because they see, and your ears because they hear"(Matthew 13:16).

In his stunning book *How to Read a Poem: And Fall in Love with Poetry,* the poet Edward Hirsch writes, "I have called the poem a soul in action through words because I want to suggest that lyric poetry provides us with a particular means of spiritual transport." He takes great pains (quoting Wordsworth) to demonstrate that much poetry has "visionary power." "It has been one of the key tasks of writers for the past two centuries to try to dramatize and unleash in their work 'visionary power,' to recall, recapture, and render those—indeed, to create—'fleeting modes/Of shadowy exultation.'"

Hirsch uses a paradoxical phrase that attempts to capture the essence of the poet's capacity: *"the immense intimacy, the intimate immensity."* For me, perhaps not for the writer, this describes both the immanence and the transcendence of God's presence, and it is what I attempt to record when I keep a life list of God Hunt sightings. These are not mundane accounts, although the mundane (battered license plates, for instance) are often used by God to bring himself near to me. They have to do with the Creator of the universe chasing after me in crazy love so that his nearness, his closeness, his within-ness can be recognized and known by me. But these faithful jottings also have to do with wonder, with awe at the overwhelming, huge vastness of a God I can never fully know or understand, One who is acting beyond my capacities to ascertain through a sovereign design, overviewing time, space, light, history and the little bands of creaturely beings that are enfolded in all that vast enormity.

Recording the God Hunt (for my whole life) helps me taste, sip and suspect something of the immense intimacy, the intimate immensity that the Holy Being, the I AM who is always present, fire-flashes into my world.

SHIMMERING SPARKS

Yesterday morning I dragged the garbage out to the street, and in the early dark of a November morning, between the garage and the street, I noticed sparklers going off in the upper quadrant of my left eye. This was new! Now, what did that mean (sparkle, sparkle)? Apart from the surprise of this phenomenon and the fact that floaters (little dots) now bobbed above the midline of my iris, there was something slightly lovely about this visual apparition. Like fireflies glimmering, like streaks of soft lightning— like my retina detaching! By the time I finally paid my full attention to this strange light, it was evening and my brother-in-law, a doctor, advised me to go to the nearby emergency room just to make sure. In fact, he offered to drive me, suspecting perhaps that I might just let it go to morning.

After two hours of waiting, filling out forms, examinations, doctors (two of them—I was sent from the emergency room over to the Wheaton Eye Clinic where an ophthalmologist was on call), then eye drops and dilating fluids, it was determined that no retinal tissue had detached. I could continue work; everything was OK.

Finding God in the everyday world is not unlike this incident. Something flashes just off the center of our vision; it draws our attention for a moment. What was that? It flashes again, a streak of shimmering sparks. At this point we have a choice. We can choose to be inattentive; we can get used to the little flashes of light, ignore them all together (as I tried to do), but this we do to our own peril. Or we can choose to attend. We can say, How lovely! We can record it, write it down, create a journal that testifies, gives witness to our eagerness to spy out the intimate immensity that it is our joy to experience. What will you choose?

Sighting

My son Joel remembers this amazing story from his days as a film student at Columbia Performing Arts School in Chicago.

I had given my final film project to a student friend to hand in to my professor so I was shocked when I received a B grade and was told that my last project hadn't been completed. Checking this out, I discovered that in my haste, I had torn off the unused film, then mistakenly given my edited film project to another student who was finishing his senior project, thinking it was the extra unused film.

When I explained this to my professor, he gave me back the processed, but blank film and said I could try to complete my project and raise my final grade. He allowed me only one session in the editing suite at an odd hour to rework my project. Now this was a commuter campus, and the students who were supposed to give me a ride into the city so that I could redo my project were two hours late in picking me up. All I could do was pray and say, "Lord, you are going to have to help me do eight hours of work in six."

However, because I was late, I ran into the film major to whom I had given what I thought was the canister of unused film. I could not have run into him earlier—"amazingly" his class was taking a short, three-minute break, and he was standing in the halls. I told him my sad tale, and we ran over to his apartment in the city. Lo and behold, he had not filmed over my project. There in his packed refrigerator freezer was my edited work—complete, unspoiled, with the torn end perfectly matching the torn end of the empty film that had been turned into the professor.

Not only did I avoid spending six hours in the editing suite, but I had the proof in the matching torn ends that the story I had told the professor was true.

9

Every Season
Is Hunting Season

> *"When I was younger," Lucian said, "and so much more confident,*
> *I was entranced with praying. I soared upwards on wings.*
> *But now I'm older, I find God through doubt as much as through belief.*
> *We search for him in the darkness. I'm full of doubts.*
> *That's what faith means."*

> MICHELE ROBERTS

While in college our youngest son, Jeremy, introduced me to one of America's alternative market economies. He and his roommate went "gleaning," a euphemism for picking the discarded garbage out of dumpsters behind major supermarket chains.

My response was exactly the same as yours might be, "What in the world are you doing? You'll get sick! Won't the police run you off?"

"Mom," my son replied (patiently, as though to a very slow senior citizen), "It's perfectly good food. And they're throwing it away. Think of the money we'll save."

My response to this (only to myself, of course) was, *Well, why do you think they're throwing it away?*

Soon I began to reconsider my negative reaction to this embarrassing garbage-picking: Pizzas still frozen. Day-old loaves of bread, only slightly squashed. Dozens of doughnuts, still on their card-board trays and wrapped protectively in cellophane. Cans with small nicks, some without labels. I myself became the recipient of twelve boxes of tossed tissues, the sides of which were only slightly bashed.

Suddenly, through my son's forays, I began to take into account the fact that we are, indeed, a shamefully wasteful society. Good foods were tossed because of expiration dates; day-old bread in certain grocery chains had to be dumped. Slight dents in cans or minor crushes in packages determined what got pitched in the dumpster. Sometimes new shipments simply meant that the old stuff needed to be moved off the shelves or out of the freezers. I began to have some confidence that if in old age there was a finan-cial collapse, we could rummage at the back of store parking lots. We certainly wouldn't starve!

Granted, I have always been a woman who furnished her home with other people's discards. Garage sales, junk shops and resale stores have been favorite haunts. At first, as a young married woman, I combed through the salvage in my parent's garage and attic, and then I discovered that I could "help" friends by taking the stuff they didn't appreciate or want. Curbside garbage days often yielded great finds. The library table in my home study, for instance, was rescued from the garbage truck and only needed a little stripping. Old wooden toolboxes serve as end tables in David's study. And a friend tells me that the Rosenthal mark and artist's signature on my garage sale, hand-painted Bavarian china indicates a real find.

Once while walking our sizable Australian Shepherd, I came across ferns dug out and stuffed in yard sacks all crumpled, wait-ing for the garbage men. Hoisting the cumbersome load, I com-pleted my walking circuit of another mile, with the dog lunging ahead and the heavy bag clutched awkwardly in my free arm. I planted the broken fronds in a wooded spot that summer and was delighted when they unfurled the next spring—twelve sturdy, green survivors.

Three of our four children have picked up the garbage-picking instincts—although I must admit some of them have taken this reclamation activity far beyond my imaginings (as with Jeremy's "gleanings"). On several occasions I've run into one son and daughter-in-law at local church bazaars and tag sales. "Mom," Joel and Laurie call out, dropping past on Saturday mornings, interrupting (with not much difficulty) my weekend plans. "There's a barn sale down the road. You should see the garden sale going on up the street. Have you dropped past the estate sale?"

My daughter Melissa and her friends have taken the gleaners' activities to new heights, elevating it to an art form. Living in the affluent towns west of the Chicago suburbs, young women all with new homes to furnish, they are determined flea market denizens. By visiting the alleys behind high-end boutiques, they have accented their houses. Often they meet one another in the middle of the night and rummage in the dark canisters with lights attached to hard hats. (This is serious stuff.) In daytime hours they attempt to be accompanied by adorable, sleeping toddlers tucked into car seats, just in case of officious inquiries. "Guess what I found?" is a frequent question, asked with barely concealed chortling glee.

Why does this surprise me when I consider that the God in whose image I am made is the consummate garbage-picker? He sees the beauty in what others view as ugly, he rescues discards from trash heaps, plucks out the rare antique from the shadows, then restores the marred and broken to surprising value. God must chortle (in fact we are told that all the angels in heavens rejoice) every time he finds and reclaims a lost human that others have counted as worthless.

The instinct to hunt is a divine instinct of which most humans partake. It is a holy urge planted in the hearts of toddlers, grade-schoolers, teens, young adults, mid-lifers and the aged. We all love to find treasures of great value.

The hunting instinct dies hard and it lasts for most of life. One of the primary hunting principles we must understand is that every season is hunting season. This is why making the God Hunt a spiritual practice is important. We must be prepared to find God in all seasons of life—spring, summer, fall, winter—and in all places of life—in the oasis, in the wilderness; in the light and in the darkness.

> Wither shall I go from thy Spirit?
>> Or wither shall I flee from thy presence?
> If I ascend to heaven, thou art there!
>> If I make my bed in Sheol, thou art there!
> If I take the wings of the morning
>> and dwell in the uttermost parts of the sea,
> even there thy hand shall lead me,
>> and thy right hand shall hold me.
> If I say, "Let only darkness cover me,
>> and the light about me be night,"
> even the darkness is not dark to thee,
>> the night is bright as the day;
> for the darkness is as light with thee."
> (Psalm 139:7-12 RSV)

WITCHES' KNOTS

I delight in giving gifts to my children. However, my family suspected that the horse I bought for my daughter's sixteenth birthday was not only for Melissa but for myself. (I suspect they were right!) Without a doubt, Melissa bore the brunt of the responsibility—feeding Lady Sundown and mucking out the stall—and received most of the pleasure, taking long rides near the small farm where we boarded the horse along with the horse of a close girlfriend (the two of them sharing stable duties). But I, too, grabbed stolen moments for relaxing rides, and I found myself filling in as stable hand at times when my daughter's schedule became prohibitive.

There is nothing quite like a cold barn on a winter day with hoarfrost on the ground outside and the warm whinnying breath of a large welcoming animal blowing clouds of vapor through a soft, warm, nuzzling nose. I loved a reckless gallop along the edge of a cornfield or walking down a sweaty horse by way of the orchard and swiping late apples from the trees.

Yet to everything there is a season. When Melissa left for college, I faced the inevitable and found some potential buyers for a first-class horse. (Believe me, this was not an easy decision; one becomes emotionally bonded to fulfilled longings!) I set aside one morning to groom Lady Sundown so she would look her best at my private horse sale. Much to my dismay, I found that she had escaped to the front pasture, which had gone to weed. Sundown's mane was a viper's nest of tangles impossibly matted together with briars and stickers.

Because I knew it would take hours to comb through the knots, my first impulse was to take scissors and cut out the tangles. I'm not much of a horsewoman, but I had been told that this particular shortcut is forbidden. One spreads the tangles and patiently combs them smooth. Better yet, a responsible owner never allows her horse to get in such a state.

So I resigned myself to a long morning, led the horse into the barn and fastened her halter to the post chains beside the grooming floor. I brushed the summer dust from her mahogany coat,

dug the mud from her hooves with a shoe pick and finally tackled
the dreadful mess of her mane. These tangles in a horse's mane
are appropriately called "witches' knots." Folklore says that
witches, out of love for chaos and pure spitefulness, tie these
time-consuming masses, and that morning I could almost believe
there was some evil design behind my tedious work.

It took me two hours to spread the knots, spray them with un-
tangling solution, then comb them smooth. Eventually I finished
and saddled Lady Sundown for one last ride. Striding her back, I
admired the results of my morning's frustrating work. A groomed
horse whose brushed and polished flanks shine in the sun is a
beautiful sight. I was glad I hadn't chopped away the tangles.
There would have been no way to hide the hacked hair, and my
impatience would have marred the beauty about Sundown I always loved.

Life is full of twisted circumstances and relationships that seem
impossible to untie—witches' knots. Many times I have found
myself thinking, *There is no end to this dilemma, no way to comb it out!* All
I have wanted to do was cut away the gnarl of impossibilities.

In her little book *IF,* Amy Carmichael has described me rather
well:

> IF I wonder why something trying is allowed, and press for
> prayer that it may be removed; if I cannot be trusted with any
> disappointment, and cannot go on in peace under any mys-
> tery, then I know nothing of Calvary love. IF I ask to be de-
> livered from trial rather than for deliverance out of it . . . if I
> forget that the way of the Cross leads to the Cross and not to
> a bank of flowers . . . so that I am surprised when the way is
> rough and think it strange, though the word is, *Think it not
> strange, Count it all joy,* then I know nothing of Calvary love.

For a long while I was a mistress of the art of praying for God to change difficult circumstances. It took years before I learned how to pray for God to change *me* in the midst of the difficult circumstances. In time I began to approach the witches' knots with (for me) an unusual kind of patience. Determination bid me comb through the tangles rather than just hack them out. What was the basic reason for this attitude shift? Without a doubt, it was the practice of daily identifying God in the ordinary events of life. The God Hunt enabled me to see his presence in the midst of the pain-filled extraordinary circumstances all humans must sooner or later face.

The God Hunt stabilizes us to cope when we find our life in knots twisted and tangled so tight we think we will never be free, when grief sits heavy on our chests, when death lifts a jeering face at us and smirks, when rejection nags, isolation taunts and rebellion mocks us. At the moments when our heads pound from stress, our hearts feel about to burst and self-disgust threatens to overwhelm us, we remember another old, sweet melody, "But God . . . but God . . . but God."

We open our prayer journals and recall the times when we made God Hunt sightings. We remember how God surprised us with intimacy, whispering "Boo!" when we had lost our way. We find that the lists of thanks recorded over years are healing balm to our battered souls. We are not abandoned; he does not delight in our torture.

Because we have developed the habit of hunting God in all seasons, we are made steadfast when we see no burning bushes, hear no still small voice, and feel twin to Job. We are given strength to comb through our tangled circumstances instead of maiming our own chance for growth by cutting out of them.

The God Hunt is one of the powerful weapons of spiritual warfare that brings about the destruction of the enemy's strongholds. The apostle Paul writes:

Though we live in the world, we do not wage war as the
world does. The weapons we fight with are not the weapons
of the world. On the contrary, they have divine power to demolish strongholds. We demolish arguments and every pre-
tension that sets itself up against the knowledge of God, and
we take captive every thought to make it obedient to Christ.
(2 Corinthians 10:3-5)

If we have been practicing the God Hunt on an everyday level,
it will become a shield and a defense when we are in the middle of
bloody spiritual conflict. Training our minds to see God in the everyday is one way to "capture every thought to make it obedient
to Christ."

We must understand, though entered into with delight and
wonder, the God Hunt is not a spiritual charade. We are not play-
acting God's drama in the world; we are lead characters in the
real-life drama of God with us. Witches' knots are often allowed
in our lives so that God can work that painful crucifixion of the
self in us that keeps us building his kingdom and not our own. It
is the work of the cross within each human heart, this breaking of
our self-will, our self-arrogance, our latent spirit of rebellion that
we must each undergo if we are to become like Christ. The God
Hunt will prepare us to learn to identify the miracle of his presence in each commonplace moment so that when times of personal crucifixion occur, we will most assuredly know that he
stands at the foot of each person's cross, that he allows suffering
so we will better identify with a suffering world.

FINDING GOD EVERYWHERE

We must also examine another hunting principle: The more you
look for something, the more you will find it everywhere. This is

the phenomenon of the trained eye. We see what we choose to look for. If you hunt for the decadent, the negative, the ugly, that is what you will see. If you search for the beautiful, the holy, the true, your eye will become practiced at finding God's loveliness everywhere.

Diane Schoemperlen's book *Our Lady of the Lost and Found* examines many historical claims to Marian visitations and apparitions throughout history. The book begins with a fictional account of a writer with whom the Virgin Mary inexplicably takes up week-long lodging. She becomes a houseguest because she's tired (frankly) and needs to rest in a quiet place where there will be no recognitions and no notoriety. The stranger is wearing a blue trench coat, white tennis shoes, a white shawl, and is a middle-aged woman with nothing remarkable about her. The author employs this fictional device, only slightly tongue-in-cheek, to examine the tension between doubt and faith (a theme I am frequently finding in contemporary secular literature).

Admittedly not much of a believer, the narrator (who must remain anonymous because she has promised the Virgin Mary not to divulge this visitation) states that she didn't much notice the cult of Mary before, but now she sees evidence of it everywhere. There are infrequent but regular television reports of sightings all over the world; a plastic religious card is taped to her beautician's mirror; a small grotto in a neighbor's yard shelters a ceramic statue of Mary, and so on.

The narrator, who is a stamp collector, also observes that even a philatelic catalog reports that in the past two decades nearly three hundred stamps using classical art reproductions of Mary have been issued by seventy-five countries. The narrator has no memory of having collected any of these imprints, but on going to her binders and flipping through the pages, she discovers that she has dozens of stamps with Raphael's Madonna on them, along with hundreds of other stamps featuring other images of Mary.

The anonymous writer states, "This new proliferation of Marys in my life would seem to give lie to the popular notion that you are most likely to find something when you're not looking for it." Unmarried, the narrator says she has noticed that this advice—Don't worry, you'll find him when you least expect it—is mostly offered as consolation to single women who are always coming up desolate and broken-hearted in their search for a mate. Then she continues, "In light of my recent experience of running into Mary everywhere I turn, it now seems to me that, much as the old notion of finding something when you're not looking for it has often been proved true, the opposite is also and equally true: you find what you are looking for. Sometimes, once your blinders have been removed, you find it over and over and over again."

How true. When I am conducting research, for instance, I suddenly find resources everywhere; articles in popular magazines, experts at dinner parties, websites on the Internet, books already on my shelves with whole chapters on the topic, and tear-sheets in old files I just happened to put aside years ago. A trained eye will see the wild bittersweet by the side of the road when everyone else in the car just zooms along unrecognizing. My son will catch the familiar flap of birds in flight while for most of us the flocks simply pass overhead unnoticed. A newly pregnant woman will suddenly notice every pregnant woman around her. An eye fixed to see will find what it is seeking.

THE FINDING BECOMES HARDER

At the same time, there is a contradiction to the hunting principle of finding what you seek: The longer you hunt, the harder it may become. God often withdraws to mature those who hunt him. It is the way God seasons us and develops our deep capacity for viewing. He tests our faith and stretches it to become an appropriate skin for our souls.

We may wrestle with doubt fearfully, honestly and tenaciously, but the wise, under trying circumstances, choose to believe God is working though they can't see how, that he is present though they can't find him, that he is speaking though his voice is silent. Our goal during these puzzling seasons is to be like those saints chronicled in Hebrews, "All these people were still living by faith when they died. They did not receive the things promised; they only saw them and welcomed them from a distance" (Hebrews 11:13-14).

The Hebrew scholar Richard Elliott Friedman chronicles what he calls "divine recession" in his book *The Disappearance of God*. Progressing through the canon of the Old Testament, from Genesis to the prophets, Friedman develops a picture of a God who "fades as he goes." The imprint of divinity that shines forth with clarity at the beginning of the history becomes dim as God withdraws, "stepping back from human beings so they will have room and the desire to step forward."

God often determines that we are ready, practiced enough in the daily hunting to experience him on retreat. Sometimes he is silent. Sometimes we can find no words to express what it is we are experiencing. During this season there seems to be no connecting between the divine and us. In *When God Is Silent,* Barbara Brown Taylor explains:

> Silence becomes God's final defense against our idolatry. By limiting our speech, God gets some relief from our description assaults. By hiding inside a veil of glory, God eludes our

projections. God deflects our attempts at control by with-drawing into silence, knowing that nothing gets to us like the failure of our speech. When we run out of words, then and perhaps only then can God be God. We have eaten our own words until we are sick of them, when nothing we can tell ourselves makes a dent in our hunger, when we are pre-pared to surrender the very Word that brought us into being in hopes of hearing it spoken again—then, at last, we are ready to worship God.

Let me share with you a somewhat mundane incident in our lives that is nevertheless symbolic of those truly hellish passages that seem to have no end, those times when we feel we will never reach safety and we cannot hear what it is we should do.

For a month and a half we'd been having some trouble with the clutch on our Honda. On two occasions (while I was driving, of course) the manual transmission jammed. The second of these instances occurred while I was laboriously stopping and starting in backed up traffic on the ramp leading to the tollbooth outside O'Hare airport in Chicago. I was scheduled to pick up a friend on Friday evening at 6:30. At 7:10 I finally made it through the toll plaza, noted the acrid odor of some overheating mechanism, and coaxed myself through traffic at the top speed of twenty miles per hour to finally reach the arrival gate at United Airlines. Much to my relief, I saw my friend waiting patiently as she had been in-structed to do, on the second concrete platform outside exit 3C.

On Friday nights O'Hare airport is ordinarily a merciless jungle with arrivals and departures vying for curb space, cheeky taxi drivers taking untoward traffic risks and city tow trucks waiting to pounce on anyone who parks curbside to check inside and see if the awaited flight has landed. This is all orchestrated by particular types of Chicago cops who are deliberately selected (I am convinced) for their abrasive, obstinate and pugnacious personalities.

But this Friday was the Friday after Thanksgiving Day. O'Hare was practically empty. I explained my dilemma to my friend who put her suitcases in the trunk; I notified the Chicago policeman standing ten feet from my car as to my car's vehicular disability. He, much to my amazement, was kind and sympathetic. (And in a noticeable German accent he gave me advice, "Lady, get an American-made car!")

For years David has bought Christmas tree ornaments for our children's trees (each around a certain theme), and now he collects miniature ornaments for the grandchildren. The hardest ornaments to find are lambs for our daughter, Melissa. While driving one day he noticed a sign for a Christmas shop that was two miles off the major highway. Because he had a little extra time, he exited the highway, went to the store, and found seven adorable lamb ornaments—all in the one shop.

We consulted as to what I should do. I phoned home; David called a tow truck. In an hour and a half the tow arrived, the Honda was attached and hoisted, my friend and I climbed into the cab, and forty-five minutes later we were delivered to my front door. Welcome to Chicago!

For the second time that month the Honda was towed to a garage. For the second time, the mechanics could find nothing wrong with the car. It started fine the next morning, the transmission slipped smoothly in and out of gear. David concluded that I'd never learned to drive a manual clutch correctly. (He forgot that it was he, himself, who taught me how to drive a clutch car when I was sixteen, a senior in high school.) I rode the gear pedal too much, he asserted. I needed to learn to slip the clutch in and out and ease the stick shift into neutral in bumper to bumper traffic. The bill came to ninety-one dollars, and it wasn't the end of our Honda's saga.

The next time we experienced trouble, my husband (the manual transmission expert) was driving. Coming home from a restful four-day vacation in Galena, Illinois, we began to notice that the clutch was pulling on the upgrades of Galena Territory's rolling hills and that our speed was slipping—sixty miles per hour, fifty-five miles per hour, forty-five miles per hour.

When David pulled off on a toll road exit, there was a definite burning odor, and the car jammed in gear as we came to the ramp stoplight. We rushed to push the disabled Honda to the side of the road. A compassionate passerby hooked our front fender to his back fender and towed us to the nearest Amoco gas station. We crossed the street in a cold drizzle to have an unplanned early afternoon meal at the closest short-order restaurant. I worked on a crossword puzzle. David walked across the parking lot to a Hallmark store and did some Christmas shopping.

In short, we were waiting for the car motor to cool. Sure enough, in an hour the Honda ran like a dream, and we made it to the first tollbooth. After that we labored in agony all the rest of the way. Drive for ten minutes. Stop and cool for ten minutes. Chug along in traffic with our hazard lights blinking. Pull over onto the shoulder with cars whizzing by.

The weather chilled degree by degree as the day kept slipping away. At the next toll, David went to call a tow truck, but returned because he couldn't read the phone book numbers since he hadn't taken his glasses. He decided to keep driving down the highway where two miles later we were forced to pull over and cool down.

Cool down in several ways, actually. David and I have styles of stress management that are diametrically opposed. He ducks his head and plunges through all obstacles, sometimes without an appropriate analysis of the consequences. I sit, consider my options, call in consultation, miss some opportunities to be sure—but I don't take unnecessary chances with my life or my well being. Needless to say, this nightmarish journey home, in the gathering dark and the icy rain, did not bring out the best elements in our marital relationship.

Finally we pulled off in Marengo, Illinois, where there were huge truck stops and service stations. We were certain we would find some tow trucks, but the only

In a painful downscaling process at Mainstay Ministries, we had to release eight staff members. Several months later we received a note from one of the women. She thanked us for the months without work, saying that God had used it to give her rest and had met her in profound ways because of the extended "retreat." She had enjoyed getting her daughter ready for college without the stress of extra responsibilities. And on the last day before her employment compensation ran out, she found a position on a local church staff working with a pastor she had worked with before. She said it felt like she was "coming home."

tow truck driver to be found had been celebrating the Chicago Bear's Sunday afternoon victory with some buddies in a nearby bar. Needless to say, he was unfit to drive. We were forty-five minutes from home, and I, beyond frustration, called the tow service in my hometown that had brought the Honda, my friend and myself home from O'Hare airport. But though I phoned three times, and lost seventy-five cents in the pay phone, no one answered. (Oh, for a direct line to Click and Clack, the riotous Magliozzi brothers, hosts of *Car Talk*, the National Public Radio Saturday morning show.)

In wretched moments like these all you want to do is get home. David decided the car had cooled enough and could get us, limping to be sure, to our house. Reluctantly I climbed into the untrustworthy vehicle. We gave it one more go, gear slipping all the way to the Elgin tollbooth that became our final Donnybrook. David exited and stopped at a gas station where the people were cooperative. Pete's Tow came, loaded us into the cab and toted us the half-hour to home, where we collapsed in a frenzy of relief. A trip that should have taken two and a half hours had taken us seven and a half hours to drive, and we spent another fifty-six bucks on the tow truck!

Sometimes we are in the middle of nightmarish journeys where we would give everything if we could just wake up. We are in desperate straits—the room with no door, the clutch that is slipping, the life that is stalling. Imminent disaster looms—and because we have not been listening, have not developed a cultivated lifetime of intimacy, we cannot hear the voice of God in these trying circumstances. There seems to be no rescue service available, no matter how much we seek help. We are strangers in the world, with no safe place.

Let me speak to you from the experience of my life—where there have been truly hellish passages. You will reach safety. God has not abandoned you. He is communing in silence, no better, as silence. If we have developed the habit of hunting for God in the everyday world (think of those tangible stacks—thirty years of prayer journals), then when the finding seems to get hard, we will have evidence of his work. We will have developed a practical knowledge of his loving care. We will have written down the daily findings, the trail marks, the stones that lead us along the path, the records of footmarks and fingerprints of the divine. We will have learned how to read the metaphors in life and have become practiced at turning them into holy meaning.

Then when the clutch begins to go, when terminal disease ravages us, when we lose our life savings, we will choose to turn in faith, we will intentionally trust, we will open our eyes wider and wait and wait and wait until he determines that the rigorous discipline needed to grow our souls has been accomplished.

Do not be surprised if one day, after years of hunting and finding him almost with each breathbeat, the finding becomes harder. This is often the way God works with those he loves. Do not be afraid, you will still be able to say, in the silence and in the darkness, "Look and see what I have found!" Every season—even the ones where God is silent—is hunting season.

Sighting

Pastor Roger Haber from Middleboro, Massachusetts, writes one of his most memorable God Hunt sightings:

A few years ago I was worn out and burned out as a pastor. There was a ranch devoted to renewal for people in the pastorate that our family would often go to for family breaks. Normally reservations had to be made months in advance, but one afternoon I called up the ranch and said, "I know this is probably impossible, but by any chance would you have something available this weekend for my wife and me?"

The woman replied, "You won't believe this, but we just had something open up, and we'd love for you and your wife to come."

Going away that weekend renewed my strength and energy— and was part of the discipline I have developed in looking for God's "fingerprints" on my life every day.

WALKING IN A HERO'S SHOES

Spiritual life begins to decay when we
fail to sense the grandeur of what is eternal in time.

RABBI HESCHEL

In *Orthodoxy* G. K. Chesterton wrote, "We have all read in scientific books, and indeed, in all romances, the story of the man who has forgotten his name. This man walks about the streets and can see and appreciate everything; only he cannot remember who he is. Well, every man is that man in the story. Every man has forgotten who he is. . . . We are all under the same mental calamity; we have all forgotten our names. We have all forgotten what we really are."

In the film *The Majestic,* Peter Appleton (played by actor Jim Carrey) is a Hollywood screenwriter during the days of the McCarthy congressional hearings on un-American activities. A car accident leaves him suffering from amnesia, and he lands in Lawson, California, where the townsfolk mistakenly believe he is one of their own heroes, Luke Trimble, returned miraculously home. Luke was declared missing in action during the Second World War and was posthumously awarded a Medal of Honor for carrying eight wounded fighting men to safety. For a while Peter Appleton, who by his own admission is a man not given to "great convictions," has a chance to walk in a true hero's shoes. He experiences what it is like to be the center of the regards, the hopes, and the love of a whole community that still mourns sixty-two of its own men who died fighting for the cause of freedom. He courts (and falls in love with) Luke's childhood sweetheart, an idealist who has just passed her bar exam and holds to high constitutional standards.

In time Peter's memory returns, and he is subpoenaed to appear before the committee investigating un-American activities. His lawyer informs him that a deal has been struck. If he confesses and renounces his communist past (of which he is innocent) and names other sympathizers, he will be free to go. Otherwise, a jail sentence awaits him. Peter is tempted to accept the deal, but at the last minute he dramatically refuses to purge himself of past Communist sympathies (since there were none), or to name any names. On national television he reminds the members of the congressional committee that the last war was fought to preserve the very freedoms they seem to be bent on destroying. Before a nation the young man credits the people of Lawson for teaching him the lessons of living for a cause larger than one's own self.

Are you one of those strangers who has forgotten your true name? Do you pass from day to day, week to week, year to year, and none of the seasons are hunting season? Have you spent a long time traveling in the wrong direction? Did some terrible act or choice incarcerate you in a room with no door? Are you so far from the practice of listening that you can no longer remember the sound of his voice when he calls you in the moments?

During those times in our lives when the seasons turn sour, when we are lost, when despite all our valiant efforts we can't get home again and there seems to be no one to help us; when we can't recognize the voice of that One calling us to play, when we are dislocated psychologically and we have no memory of who it is we are any more, how is it that (as Scripture says) "we come to our senses"?

LOST IDENTITY

Our displacement from our true identity comes not only from the hurtful ways people have treated us, causing us to costume ourselves in protective personality camouflage, but for many, life has forced us to function with false identities. Somehow we have been assigned a role given by others that is not true to the calling God has planned for us. We are stuck in a lie. Perhaps we failed at one time in our life (or succeeded wildly) and now we must endure the effects of a past error we cannot overcome or glory in past accomplishments we have outgrown.

Think of how frequently Scripture tells of name changes (and consequent identity changes) that seem to be inherent in the lives of those who dramatically meet with God: Saul was renamed Paul; Jacob became Israel; Abram became Abraham; Gideon became Jerubbal; Moses changed Hoshea's name to Joshua—the study is extensive. In Revelation, God declares, "I will give a white stone, and on the white stone is written a new name that no one knows except the one who receives it" (2:17 NRSV).

For decades I worked at creating an identity as a writer. "What do you do?" people would ask. "Oh, I write; I'm a writer." This was no fantasy; I had countless broadcasts, over twenty books and who knows how many articles to prove it. In addition, national awards, a place on bestseller lists, membership in literary associations (some I had helped to establish), credentialed this identity. This worked for a while—for about twenty years—but then I came to a crossroads where the divinely ordered circumstances of my life forced me to look at the fact that my basic identity was not what I had been framing.

In fact, this was a false self I had unwittingly assumed, pulled over my head and was wearing. The cloak hiding my true identity needed to be cast aside. Talk about terror. If not a writer, then who was I? The Lord came to my assistance (totally without my invitation, by the way) by stripping me of everything that had

In order to travel in Europe we ordered Eurail passes in the States. We left the States on December 27, and I had a nagging feeling we should get seat reservations. Most travel guides report that a tourist can simply get on the train without reservations, but one or two traveler's articles had recommended purchasing seat reservations at low cost, just to be safe. When we reached our first major city in Europe, we made our way to the Eurail counter and begin to request reservations for the days ahead. We were traveling over the extended European holiday season, and we just "happened" to get the last seats available.

I am always sorry when I fail to pay attention to those inner nudges. They invariably come from another source than my own human wisdom.

formed my writerly sense of whom I was. I howled and wailed, had temper-tantrums and screamed in the dark. I did not like standing naked with my deformities showing, but then the God who is always present began to whisper my true name. First, he whispered it in silence, of course, and I couldn't hear. Then he slapped my hands when I tried to surreptitiously pull closer the cloak I had been wearing to cover my raw nakedness. This felt uncharitable and unfeeling. I was exposed to hail and cold winds, to sun-scorch, bug bites and distressing humidity. But eventually, after years, in the silence, in the silence that is God (he has all the time in the universe), I am beginning to understand my true identity (the name has yet to be spoken to me). This identity has something to do with that inner word I hear over and over, day in and day out, *Attend. Look and listen. Watch and see. Pay attention.*

God, it seems, is always attempting to call us to our true identity in him. Through midget crosses and minor crucifixions, God is helping me to overcome the labels or expectations wrongfully placed upon me. He is teaching me to walk in a true hero's shoes, to live for a little while in the shadow of a Hero who has laid down his life for his friends. He is using the Holy Spirit to continuously frame me in the image of the Lord Jesus Christ, who demonstrated unquestionable authentic authority and at the same time, astounding natural humility.

WALKING IN THE HERO'S SHOES

In identifying God's work, we learn more of his nature. By marking the daily paths with stacked stones, we remember to attend. When we pay attention, we become more familiar with the nature of the One we are sighting. When we begin to know the One we are looking to see (at the same time that he is looking for and finding us), we begin to desire to become like him. When we become like him, we begin to discover wondrously who it is he has created us to be. "You chart the path ahead of me and tell me where to stop and rest./Every moment you know where I am./You both precede and follow me" (Psalm 139:3, 5 NLT).

"Beloved, we are God's children now" (some of our true identity is revealed here on earth); "it does not yet appear what we shall be" (we do not really know what our heavenly nature shall be like), "but we know that when he appears" (at the end of time as we understand it) "we shall be like him, for we shall see him as he is" (1 John 3:2 RSV). The apostle is talking about a future eschatology, yet this principle of becoming like what we are seeking fills the rest of his epistles. We are to walk in the light and love of God, and the obedience of that walk will make us like our heavenly Father and his son, Jesus Christ.

The daily God Hunt helps us to sight the one we are seeking to know; and in the very act of continual sighting, when this becomes a lifetime habit, we will become like what we are seeking. This principle applies across the board. If it is money you want, then you will become a money-first person. If it is power, then you will find a way to squirm and worm yourself into positions of influence, be they large or small. You might want to ask yourself, however: Is this who I want to be? Beware! You will become like whatever it is you are seeking! Will I be happy being a power-monger? A greedy financier? Make sure your life hunt, the hours you devote to searching for that most important treasure, is what you want to become.

Lost yourself? Suffering from amnesia? Then walk for a while in a Hero's identity. How did Christ deal with the dangerous idealizations that attempted to pin him to a false identity? What did he do about those religious authoritarians who were always attempting to devalue him? How did he handle the wounds that eventually took his life? It is only by taking on our Hero's identity that we will understand how people who are less than heroes should behave. As the Scripture teaches, "Therefore be imitators of God, as beloved children. And walk in love, as Christ loved us and gave himself up for us" (Ephesians 5:1-2 RSV).

The God Hunt is another name for the old spiritual discipline called practicing the presence of Christ. Whatever we practice is what we will become proficient at being. If we practice the piano, we will become a musician. If we discipline ourselves to excel in gymnastics, we will become a gymnast. If we become proficient at working in the garden, we will become a gardener. If we practice Christ, we will become a Christ-one.

Sometimes when we're trying to get home, we keep shouting like the little kid who has lost his mother in a crowded place. (Remember that frantic panic?) "Ma," he cries, and before she has a chance to answer, he screams again. "Ma! Ma! MA!" She's been answering the whole time, "I'm here. I'm coming. I'll be right there!" But all the child can do is keep screaming, and the more he screams, the more he can't hear her, and the more panic squeezes his little psyche in monstrous paroxysms. She will soon swoop him up in her arms, kiss the frightened child and wipe away the tears on the sweat-streaked face.

Like the mother finding her panicked child, God also says, "I'm here. I'm close by. I'm coming. Just be still, I'll show you where you are and where I am." Stop screaming when you are stuck, lost, or can't get home. Listen. Listen deeply. Look around you. What you are seeking is closer than you think. God is in the things that happen to us. He doesn't cause them, that is often of our own doing, but he is near. He is always rushing to help us.

The Majestic ends when Peter Appleton decides to take the train back to Lawson. He calls the woman he has come to love and tells her he needs to return the borrowed medal of honor, a last letter to her from Luke Trimble on the battlefield and her book on the American Constitution. "I have a question to ask you," he says. "Meet me at the train station. If you're not there, I will leave the package with the station master and just go on."

When his train pulls into the station, a band is waiting as well as a mob of townspeople Appleton has come to know and respect. A banner reads, "WELCOME HOME AGAIN!" Another shouts, "LAWSON'S FAVORITE SON!" The people of Lawson, knowing Peter's true identity, still give him a hero's welcome. Soon he finds the one face in the crowd he is searching for, and she is smiling. This is the place where he belongs.

Every time we hear that voice of the One who calls our name and recognize it, we come home. Turning around, we find him already facing us. Awakening our souls unnumbered times a day, we enter rest. Correcting minor deviations, our work proceeds; the tunnel is joined, the cupola is finished. Going the right way, we see the shining towers and spires of the enchanted city. We all, every man and woman, are Lawson's favorite; for we have learned to walk in the shoes of a true Hero. We know more and more of who we are; this is where we belong.

TESTIFY

Another way we find our identity is in the way we construe words. If we speak forth something frequently enough, we can become it. In addition to seeking and finding God in the everyday of our lives, we want to speak about those discoveries. We want to be comfortable with saying, "I saw God today. Let me tell you about it" or "I had a God Hunt sighting today" or "I spied God this morning, or this afternoon, or yesterday evening." More than internal reflection, this continual articulation reinforces our experience. For instance, an actor memorizing lines from a play speaks the words out loud, over and over. The player needs more than an inner repetition, in some way the outer physical ear needs to hear, test the nuances, edit the volume of delivery, aid in the mnemonic exercise of telling the words forth, over and over.

I saw God today. I attended. So I tell it forth. The more I tell it forth, the more my identity becomes what I tell. I am not a writer: I am a God-seeker, a God-finder, a God-showing-it-forth person, a God-haunted lover.

To say, "Look what I found!" helps us concretize the divine incidents, to make them firm not only in our own consciousness, but in the consciousness of others. This is called testifying, or speaking our witness. We are telling the truth in a world filled with calumny, a society built on lies. "In testimony, people speak truthfully about what they have experienced and seen, offering it to the community for the edification of all," says Thomas Hoyt Jr. in an essay, which is part of the book *Practicing Our Faith.* Hoyt explains that society is based on truth-telling covenants so endemic that we often overlook their powerful societal implications. From courts of law to truth-in-advertising, to parents questioning their children, to the trust commitment between spouses, to business practices, to accounting regulations, to security exchanges—truth-telling is absolutely necessary to keep the fabric of our lives together from unraveling.

We must speak the truth, as hard as it is at times, and testify honestly. This translates into integrity in our character. The more we practice truth-telling, the more we become truth-tellers. We begin to think truthfully, live truthfully. The philosopher Paul Ricoeur applies testimony to "words, works, actions, and to lives which attest to an intention, an inspiration, an idea at the heart of experience and history which nonetheless transcends experience and history."

When we see God in the everyday and tell somebody, we are attesting to a momentary divine encounter that transcends our particular experience. The I AM THAT I AM has met us in some particular way, but this is only part of the incomprehensible nature of divine reality. The words we speak catch the flaming leaf on the burning shrub that is part of all the God-emblazoned fire-filled holy firmness that is everywhere, all over.

As we speak forth, we tell, and truth forms our own selves and also the community around us. Thomas Hoyt tells us:

> The practice of testimony requires a person to commit voice and body to the telling of the truth. It guards the integrity of personal and communal life, as much on the grand stage of history as in the small exchanges of home. Today, living in a world where falsehood is strong, we need to support one another as we rise to bear witness, speaking the truth about what we have seen and heard.

If you share what you are sighting, other hunters will tell their tales to you. John Schwartz, my hunting consultant in India, said that the best part of hunting was sitting around the campfire at night telling tall stories to one another, laughing, then slipping into the accounts of one another's lives in such a way that bonding occurs between the hunters. So also, in telling our stories of hunting for God in the world, by the light of his ultimate brightness, we weave his story in such a way that all our identities are intertwined.

We humans are actually rather mute in our witness. Scripture says that all nature is proclaiming the glory of God. Hear the witness in Jaroslav Vajda's hymn "God of the Sparrow, God of the Whale."

> God of the sparrow, God of the whale,
> God of the swirling stars,
> How does the creature say Awe?
> How does the creature say Praise?
>
> God of the earth-quake, God of the storm,
> God of the trumpet blast,
> How does the creature say Woe?
> How does the creature say Save?

God of the rainbow, God of the cross,
God of the empty grave,
How does the creature say Grace?
How does the creature say Thanks?

God of the hungry, God of the sick,
God of the prodigal,
How does the creature say Care?
How does the creature say Life?

God of the neighbor, God of the foe,
God of the pruning hook,
How does the creature say Love?
How does the creature say Peace?

God of the ages, God near at hand,
God of the loving heart,
How do your children say Joy?
How do your children say Home?

SPEAK IT FORTH

One crisp spring morning David and I canceled all appointments and slipped away to the Garfield Park Conservatory on Chicago's West Side. (Designed by architect Jens Jensen in 1908, it still remains the largest extant greenhouse in North America.) The reason for our playing hooky was to see the Dale Chihuly exhibition: *Chihuly in the Park: A Garden of Glass.*

For those unfamiliar with the glassworks of this artist, it is impossible to describe the impact hundreds of transparent glass forms have when exhibited among the foliage in the glass conservatory. Chihuly's creations are described as "delicately organic to the extravagantly florid . . . the full drama of superlative glass-blowing in which the molten material is taken to the furthest extremes of size and stretchability." Indeed, some pieces, in themselves made of hundreds of blown glass forms, were as large as the palm trees they complemented. Or they floated as huge opaque balls, luminescent, on the surface of pools. There was an amazing juxtaposition between these extravagant glass creations and the tranquil conservatory, which exuded warmth, moisture, the verdant smell of soil and the sounds of hydrating systems spraying leaves and fountains and pools.

At every turn we were caught by another exquisite creation, nature showing off the glass and the glass proclaiming nature. "Exuberance is beauty," said William Blake, and Chihuly had certainly put on a show to demonstrate this. Vibrant colors contrasted with the organic green, and wild artificial forms highlighted the outrageous plant life, causing us to see the familiar in new ways. Blown glass was hung, planted and tucked beneath; it sprouted wildly, bloomed from its fixed state, reached toward the ceiling, and tossed light. "Did you see this one?" David and I called to one another. "Oh, look here. Isn't this wonderful? Isn't this amazing?"

I just wanted to stop, sit and stare, stay for lunch and dinner, watch the daylight overhead turn to starlight, lie down on my stomach, knees bent, ankles crossed, chart the dawn's rising, smell the earth and watch the living quality of the inanimate glass—all exhibited under overarching domes of glass! Here was grandeur in time.

We went home, called friends and talked to family, mentioning over and over the Chihuly exhibit. "Take the children," we said. "Take a date. You will not be disappointed. You will not see anything like this again."

We testified to the beauty. We told others. We spoke forth the breathtaking wonder of the exhibit. Later in the Cincinnati Museum of Art I noticed a large extravagant, wondrous glass-blown chandelier hanging in the entry hall. *That's a Chihuly,* I thought. And I told my friend. (See how this knowing has become a part of me?)

Have you lost your identity, misplaced it somehow? Begin walking in a true hero's shoes. See the footprints on the ground; stand in them and size yourself. Gaze long at the exuberance of his beauty intervening in the everyday. Speak it forth. Tell somebody. Track him. He is tracking you. I promise you will find yourself again.

Recently I was struck with the reality of this intimacy. Thinking about Christ's words from John 15:4, "Remain in me, and I will remain in you," I began to consider what this could possibly mean to me. I thought about the apostle John with his head on the breast of Christ during the Last Supper before our Lord's betrayal, trial and torture. When your head is that close to the body of another person, you can hear the heartbeat, feel the pulse; you are aware of breath being inhaled and exhaled.

I realized that when I pray, I should be resting my head against the breast of this One. I should hear the heartbeat, feel the feathery aspiration on my face. Not only this, I remembered Christ's words from John 14:20, "I am in my Father, and you are in me, and I am in you." When my head is on the breast of Christ, my being tucked within his embrace, Christ's head is on the breast of God, hearing the pattern of the divine heartbeat. The Son is enfolded within the embrace of the Father, and I within the embrace of the Son. *Breathe,* they say to me. And in prayer we breathe together; in and out, in and out. *You and I are the same. Don't be afraid. Together. Breathe with me.*

Listen to God breathing, crawl close to his heart. Are you suffering from spiritual amnesia? Listen, listen—thadum . . . thadum . . . thadum . . . thadum. He is that near, that imminent. How is it possible that we cannot find him?

Sighting

Katherine Gagayan from Bangkok, Thailand, tells about her senior
year in college when there was no money to pay for her schooling.
Her father had instructed her to return home, but she was
determined to find a way to finish school and receive her bachelor's
degree. If only she could find one of the faculty families who took
students into their homes, but with the term only one week away,
those boarding opportunities were filled. Katherine spent a day in
prayer and fasting.

Making her way across campus at sunset, she came upon one of
the staff on horseback–"Papa Javier"–
so called because of his
kindliness. The rider paused
his horse to chat a little,
and the student told him
about her search for a
way to stay in school.
"Oh," he replied. "Stop by
my house tomorrow and let's
talk with my wife."

The next morning the young woman visited the couple, and they explained to her that they were allowed to house three students. There was still one slot left that they would gladly reserve for her.

Grateful, Katherine then mentioned how fortunate she was to meet Papa Javier the night before. To her amazement he said, "I didn't meet you last night." Though she reminded him of their encounter, he insisted it hadn't happened.

Reconstructing the meeting in her memory, the young woman recalled that because it was almost dark and the rider was wearing a hat, she had never clearly seen his face, only the shape of his strong body on horseback. Katherine could only conclude that God had cared about her dilemma enough to send an angelic messenger to guide her to the loving care of the Javier family.

❖

II

GATHERING DAY

And he will send his angels and gather his elect from the four winds, from the
ends of the earth to the ends of the heavens.

MARK 13:27

Years ago early one day in September, I woke curiously alive.
What a beautiful gathering morning! I collected baskets and
buckets to fill the back of the station wagon, found gardening
gloves to protect my hands and rummaged for clippers in the
kitchen catch-all drawer. Heading off to meet my friends, Lou
and Mary, I kept thinking, *This day we are going to gather, and it is a per-*
fect, wonderful fall morning.

Lou and Mary are artists in creating natural arrangements.
They weave vines, dried flowers and pods into delicate wall hang-
ings, wreaths, swags and baskets. Unlike those who put together
paint-by-number compositions, dull duplicates that look like all
the others in arts and crafts booths, these two are not afraid to
leave the wildness in the work. Creation's oddities are respected
and integrated into their designs.

I was eager to gather with these practiced field hands, who
identify the weeds by name, know where to find them and have
enough experience to understand which methods are best for
drying which plants. Naturalists, people with literacy in the lore
of the world, wake dormant yearnings in me.

We met at Mary La Frenz's home outside St. Charles, Illinois. Her A-frame house is planted atop one of the few ridges of high land we have in this part of the state. Hills actually loll down and away from her deck. Mary's basement is neatly festooned with hanging bunches: rich colored statice, yellow yarrow. Lids were lifted from barrels to show off the heads of zinnias peeking from layers of desiccants. Dried flowers were being designed for a wedding; the bridal bouquet was made of wild quinine and wispy baby's breath, and everything was tied with yards of cream satin ribbons. Wispy strands, now cooled, thread like spider's tracings through her swags and wreaths.

We walked to Mary's drying shed down a path where moss grows, up the porch into the dark interior. Here were more wreaths in the making, more hanging bunches, more hydrangea blooms air drying, bundled sheaves of grasses. (Frankly, I am envious. I covet a laboratory of my own, a studio to house my experiments in form.)

We started our gathering in the fields that stretch westward beyond the farthest edge of these suburbs. The day was grand: blue skies, white full clouds, the sun striking color upon all growing things. I was dressed in old jeans, field boots and a long-sleeved shirt—anything to keep scratches from bloodying me. Lou, however, wore shorts, her legs and arms berry-brown, like a child golden from summer's favor. We plunged into the tall weeds and grasses, the ground crunching with each step. I began collecting purple coneflower. Already field-dried, the petals had fallen, and the rich, burgundy-brown heads stood black against the bright light. Some centers were swollen to walnut size, topping tall on proud stems. I scrolled a middle finger across the porcupine texture.

I loved the milky quinine in Mary's basement; she knew where it grew. We followed through a tree windbreak into open pasture.

The heads of creamy umbels were quickly gathered into rubber bands, and my baskets were laden with the morning's booty: amber-brown wands of common mullein; bound bergamot, the leaves fragrant and ever more so when crushed; clusters of wild yarrow, now a warm golden brown. Two of my baskets were already full.

The only way I can describe my feelings is to say that I was purely exultant. This was undiluted pleasure. Imagine! To have *time* to walk across the land, to feel it uneven but substantial beneath my shoes. Imagine! To have time *enough*; nothing interrupts me, no one demands my attention. Surely the nature of Christ the Creator shows forth in all these things, in this grand and perfect day. What a thought! The print of the originator is on these pods. Dust them for identification, his fingerprints show forth!

I wanted to caress these growing things. I wanted to hold them the way a parent tucks an infant's chubby foot in the palm of her hand and draws it to the mouth to kiss. And I felt spiritually responsive, alive to all that can be read in these fields, along these paths, in these tall blooms readying themselves for hibernation. To be as unself-consciously alive as these growing things! To be as completely who God has made me to be as they are completely what God has made them to be!

I watched the passing light, its effect on the stems, on the russet lace of chawed and middle-aging leaves, on the hills (such as we Illinoisans have), on the trees staining slightly umber rose, but mostly still green. In her book *A Natural History of the Five Senses*, author Diane Ackerman writes, "We think of our eyes as wise seers, but all the eye does is gather light." And that is what my eye was doing. I was gathering light. My eyes were gathering the spilled shards of light, light on the curled dock, its lanceolated leaves twisting and drying, its thousand beads turned a rich, red brown. I was gathering the light on the nodding thistle, bleached wheat-gold, flat-domed, with a velvet butter center.

The light was so stunning I can understand that it is also danger-ous. Intoxicating, addictive, blinding, it can interfere with a day's se-rious study, with solemn work. El Greco, the great painter who made his final home in Toledo, Spain, developed, like many geniuses in late age, stunning spiritual qualities in his canvases. The legend goes that he was found working in the dark in his studio. When ques-tioned, he explained that "daylight blinded the light within."

El Greco was right. Light can be dangerous—the dazzling light of the exterior world with its marquee shades and variations, and the light of the inner world, difficult to interpret for oneself and to translate to others. "The true light that gives light to every man was coming into the world. He was in the world, and though the world was made through him, the world did not recognize him. He came to that which was his own, but his own did not receive him" (John 1:9-11). A seer must learn how to view the light, how to gather it, then what to do with it. The God Hunt may begin with the simplicity and innocent credulity of a child, but it can be-come complex and complicated the more we understand of it.

GATHERING LIGHT

Most of us traverse this world seeing very little. The natural world rarely shakes us. We do not see it; we only glance at it. To see the physical world, to really observe, takes time. We must sit on the porch and mull the moments, walk in the rain and gather mud on our boots. The world cannot be viewed well from a speeding car, though we fool ourselves into thinking that we have "seen" the mountain, the river, or the prairie. To see the world, we must climb the mountain, sit beside the river and walk in the prairie. We must see the world closely enough to learn what to call it. Then we must pause beside it to consider what it means. Frederick Turner once wrote that Thoreau learned to look "so deeply into a natural fact that at last it reveals its hidden spiritual dimension." Gathering days force me to see and to honor the beauty of what I habitually ignore or neglect.

These principles are also true when seeing with the eyes of the soul. Seeing takes time, courage and humility. So few of us know how to gaze outward or inward or upward with spiritual insight. We are blinded to the physical beauty around us that points toward the truths of the spiritual beauties to which we are also sightless. Somehow, there is a synergy between the two; learning to see in either arena, the natural world or the spiritual world, can be a practice discipline for apprehending the other. The early church father John of Damascene once explained that "visible images are often symbols of the invisible realities, so that through the material things we gain a certain idea of the immaterial realities." Poems about God are often written in the material firmament (as Annie Dillard has expressed in her book by the title *Holy the Firm*).

So we must become gatherers, diligent hunters. We must learn to gather light spiritually and to take care lest it stun us beyond reason's ability to understand it. We must learn to gather the light of Christ as it is reflected off other Christians. We must learn to honor them, even though their Christian forms, most often different from our own, are not quite what we desire. We must learn to understand that they shed his brilliant presence in the darkness.

We must learn to gather light with a rigorous and dedicated study of theology. We must watch the light shine from the pages of Scripture and not become arrogant in our own learning; the study is to inform and to change and to recreate us, not simply for the sake of intellectual prowess. We must catch sight of the match struck, tracking an incandescent line by the Holy Spirit (both knowable and inscrutable) through the dark woods of our living. We must learn to live with the paradoxes of seeing that are like the paradoxes of the incarnation: "The one who was invisible becomes visible."

We must also gather light from our life experiences. Frederick Buechner advises us in *Now and Then* that we must listen to our lives.

> If God speaks to us at all other than through such official channels as the Bible and the church, then I think that he speaks to us largely through what happens to us.... If we keep our hearts and minds open as well as our ears, if we listen with patience and hope, if we remember at all deeply and honestly, then I think we come to recognize, beyond all doubt, that, however faintly we may hear him, he is indeed speaking to us, and that, however little we may understand of it, his word to each of us is both recoverable and precious beyond telling.

On that September morning a rare and delicately balanced moment embraced me. The outward, material activities mated with the inward, spiritual realities. I was gathering weeds, but I now know that I was gathering other things as well. I was gathering time, certainly; I was gathering experiences, thoughts. But mostly I was gathering metaphorical meanings. For instance, I realized that I am always being gathered myself (being "fetched" as Deuteronomy 30:4 describes it). "If any of thine be driven out unto the outmost parts of heaven, from thence will the LORD thy God gather thee, and from thence will he fetch thee: And the LORD thy God will bring thee into the land ... and will circumcise thine heart and the heart of thy seed, to love the LORD thy God with all thine heart" (Deuteronomy 30:4-6 KJV). God is the gatherer, the originator of gathering days, with a primary impulse to always bring us back to himself. Before that September day I had never thought of him in this way. Christ told so many hunting and gathering parables because his kingdom has much to do with searching out the treasure, with arduous hunts, with exultant findings. He, and his Father, and the Holy Spirit (we must never forget) are the consummate gatherers. "And he will send his angels and gather his elect from the four winds, from the ends of the earth to the ends of the heavens" (Mark 13:27).

GOD IN THE UNDERBRUSH

As the weather began to shift that September morning, the air cooling and clouds filling the sky, I began wondering how Lou and Mary see. How do they see that bittersweet vine—without its biennial berries? How do they know the fluffy boneset would hang dry for bouquets and arrangements? How do they distinguish the snakegrass in the stand of weeds? Mary and I talked about seeing. I've taken a course in fungi identification at a local arboretum, and my eye is sensitized to bracken ledged on a tree trunk, the filigreed lichen on the forest floor.

Suddenly I saw a white glimmer in the forest half-light. "Oh, look, a puffball!" I cried. "They're edible!" Gently I twisted the puffball off its base. A mushroom delicacy, washed and sliced and cooked in butter—one by itself is large enough to make an entire meal for several diners.

"How did you see that?" Mary asked, laughing at me.

"How could I miss it? It's the size of a football!" Sighting puffballs is hardly a feat—it fairly glows in the dim woods, but nevertheless, we all find what we have been trained to see.

We see what we are looking for. We will find the object of our hunt. We will discover it in the world or in our daily lives; we will find it in one another. Consequently, we must make certain that what we give ourselves to gather in our lives is worthy of the hunting and discovering. A friend, enormously successful in her field, said to me recently, "Nothing I have done really matters." I want to live a life dedicated to the seeking, the finding and the showing forth of God in my days. I want to make sure that everything I do matters.

Going on the God Hunt is exactly like this. Our trained eye catches glimpses of him in the underbrush of our days, and we begin gathering evidences that show his concern, his involvement and his activity in our lives. "Look!" we cry. "It is he! It is he! I found him!" The natural world, the created world, is a place where theologians as poetic as King David, as prophetic as Isaiah, as parabolic as Christ, as doctrinaire as the apostle Paul, proclaim that God's personality is in his handiwork. We must learn to live our lives finding the divine in our experiences and in our days.

Recently a friend shared a story about her child. She was driving in the rain, and the little voice from the backseat said, "Mommy, Jesus is like the windshield wipers."

"Yes," my friend responded, wondering where this was going. "In what way?"

"When we sin it is like the rain, and the wipers keep wiping it away."

"And," asked the mother, "what happens if it keeps raining?"

"If it keeps raining, Jesus keeps wiping."

This is what I mean by innocent credulity, an insouciant ability to discover meaning in the mundane, to find holy lessons in the firm, to see God surrounding us in life's happenings.

GATHERING HIS OWN

When I returned home, my station wagon was loaded with bunched pickings. Before leaving we had found carrion vine, with its solidly packed balls of blue-black berries and then, at last, the wild grapevine. Stretching tendrils were yanked from the high branches. Mary and Lou formed circlets right away, taking advantage of the malleability, stripping the fresh eaves by pulling the loops through the channel of their fists. In addition, we gathered whorled milkweed, redtop grass, field aster, tickseed, tansy—all neatly bunched with Lou's rubber bands. I could scarcely see out the back window to drive.

In the fall of 2002 we received an unexpected $5,000 check as a love gift from a church David had founded and pastored decades ago. Then we received an unusually high honorarium from a week of ministry (where we had thought we were not going to receive any honoraria at all). All together, this provision underwrote our living during an extremely difficult financial period at the ministry when I went off salary and David's paycheck was as much as five pay periods behind. In addition, during this time one of our children unexpectedly repaid a gift that I had given to help underwrite an overseas trip. God's care came to us before we knew we would need it!

I was shot full of adrenaline. I could smell the crushed oils of herbs on my fingertips. How long had it been since I gave myself a whole day to collect the world in my hands? I vowed not to let the worthy demands upon my days—child rearing, ministry and travel, being a wife and friend—pull me away from all the things that most quicken my soul. "Life is a spell so exquisite that everything conspires to break it," wrote Emily Dickinson. And in truth, sadly, though I try not to, this is a vow I break again and again.

After failure I retrench, determined, despite the hardships, not to lose wonder over this life that has been given to me. Charles Baker writes in an essay about fiction published in *DoubleTake* magazine, "So, finally, we arrive at wonder, which, for me, is at the bottom level, the ground floor, of stillness. Wonder is at the opposite pole of worldliness, just as stillness is at the opposite pole from worldly action. Wonder puts aside the known and accepted, along with sophistication, and instead serves up an intelligent naiveté." I am holding on to intelligent naiveté. I have been in God's world this morning, observing, collecting. It is a wonder. Let me be still enough to absorb the meaning of it all, to know more of it in a deeper way.

Joel, our second son, was home when I returned. To my delight, he had been laying a plywood floor in the garage attic for me, and I was grateful. We needed storage space. He laughed at my bounty (what great humor I often provide for my children) and noticed right away how smug I seemed. Yes, I said. I just had a perfect— an exquisitely perfect—day. I had been gathering.

Is this how God feels when he gathers his own—content, smug and satisfied to have done a good work, his satchels filled with live and lovely game? How beautiful are the pictures of restoration and how delighted the gatherer seems about his future plans in this passage from Jeremiah:

> "See, I will bring them. . .
>> and gather them from the ends of the earth.
> Among them will be the blind and the lame,
>> expectant mothers and women in labor;
>> a great throng will return.
> They will come with weeping;
>> they will pray as I bring them back.
> I will lead them. . . .
> They will come and shout for joy on the heights of Zion;
>> they will rejoice in the bounty of the LORD. . . .

Then maidens will dance and be glad,
    young men and old as well.
I will turn their mourning into gladness;
    I will give them comfort and joy instead of sorrow.
I will satisfy the priests with abundance,
    and my people will be filled with my bounty,"
        declares the LORD. (Jeremiah 31:8-9, 12-14)

This is a picture of a perfect, exquisite gathering day! As we hunt for God in the world, he is hunting for us. As we gather evidence of his interventions, he is gathering us.

What despair God must feel when he gathers nothing, when the harvesting yield is depleted, when the vines are fruitless! Jesus wept when he returned empty-handed: "O Jerusalem, Jerusalem . . . how often I have longed to gather your children together, as a hen gathers her chicks under her wings, but you were not willing!" (Luke 13:34).

Together Joel and I disgorged the station wagon. Joel unscrewed broom handles from the long push brooms and hung them as rods between the bicycle hooks in the ceiling. I tied bunches with string and passed them to him on the ladder, and he secured them upside down to the broomsticks. We ran out of space; the remaining bunches are strung from the runners of the open overhead garage door—it will have to stay ajar. Perhaps once the floor is laid, I can convert a quarter of the attic to my own temporary drying shed.

Later, in bed—blissful, replete, content—my mind begins to rock me to sleep by weaving analogies. If I am flushed with joy at gathering the field flowers, what a state must God be in when he "fetches" his own. Does he tread the world, sending his Spirit forth, looking for finds? Does he exclaim over each particular creation, calling out to his friends, "Oh, look, a puffball beneath the trees! Oh, wild and curling grapevines! Oh, here, apples! Taste and see!" Does he hang us up to dry so that we will become everlasting?

More striking, when he comes to gather me, will he gloat at the discovery that is my life and say, "You are exactly what I had in mind! Just what I needed to finish the bridal bouquet!" And will he smile and pluck me up?

I breathe my last prayer of the day, a personal compline: *Oh God, be always gathering me. Let me always be part of your merry restoration. Let the consolation of the festival days strike rhythm on the drum of my soul. Turn my weeping into joy. Turn my sorrows into gladness. Most of all, let me see.*

HUNTING HABITS

The grandchildren and I are making plans for the annual Easter egg hunt. One or two of them help me buy the toys (gardening tools, math puzzle books, bug boxes), and some fill the plastic eggs with nickels, dimes and quarters. The parents bring two boxes of individually packaged healthy snacks, and then the fathers hide everything in the back yard and at the edges of the woods so the children can collect their finds into the Easter baskets that hang from the laundry room ceiling, stored for Holy Saturday.

None know this, but I am building hunting habits—providing opportunities to see the bright flash of eggs and treasures hidden behind tree trunks, beside rocks. Here we train the discerning eye and evoke the wonder of the chase. "Look what I found," they cry. *I spy. I spy.*

One day, these children will teach their own children and grandchildren how to gather and how to be found by the Hunter who is always present in our seeking.

Gotcha!

Further Reading

Ackerman, Diane. *A Natural History of the Senses.* New York: Random House, 1990.

Barna, George. *The State of the Church: 2002.* Ventura, Calif.: Issachar Resources, 2002.

Bass, Dorothy C. *Practicing Our Faith: A Guide to Conversation, Learning, Growth.* San Francisco: Jossey-Bass, 1997.

Brooke, Avery, ed. *Celtic Prayers.* New York: Seabury Press, 1981.

Buechner, Frederick. *Now and Then.* San Francisco: HarperSanFrancisco, 1991.

Carmichael, Amy. *IF.* Grand Rapids, Mich.: Zondervan, 1967.

Carson, Rachel. *The Sense of Wonder.* New York: HarperCollins, 1998.

Csikszentmihalyi, Mihaly. *Flow: The Psychology of Optimal Experience.* New York: HarperCollins, 1991.

Davis, Holly. "The Sunken Cities of Egypt." <www.scicom.ucsc.edu/SciNotes/0101/egypt.html>.

de Waal, Esther. *Seeking for God: The Way of St. Benedict.* Collegeville, Minn.: Liturgical Press, 1984.

Dooley, David, ed. *The Collected Works of G. K. Chesterton.* Vol. 1. San Francisco: Harper & Row, 1977.

Downing, David C. *The Most Reluctant Convert: C. S. Lewis's Journey to Faith.* Downers Grove, Ill.: InterVarsity Press, 2002.

Edwards, Tilden. *Sabbath Time: Understanding and Practice for Contemporary Christians.* Nashville: Upper Room, 1992.

Eliot, T. S. *Choruses from "The Rock," The Complete Poems and Plays 1909–1950.* New York: Harcourt Brace Jovanovich, 1971.

Heschel, Abraham Joshua. *The Sabbath: Its Meaning for Modern Man.* New York: Noonday, 1951.

Hirsch, Edward. *How to a Read a Poem: And Fall in Love with Poetry.* New York:

Harcourt Brace & Company, 1999.

King, Ross. *Brunelleschi's Dome: How a Renaissance Genius Reinvented Architecture.* New York: Penguin, 2001.

MacDonald, George. *Diary of an Old Soul: 366 Writings for Devotional Reflection.* Minneapolis: Augsburg, 1994.

McEwan, Ian. *Atonement.* London: Vintage, 2001.

Merrill, Christopher. *From the Faraway Nearby: Georgia O'Keefe As Icon.* Reading, Mass.: Addison-Wesley, 1993.

Mulholland, Robert, Jr. *Shaped by the Word: The Power of Scripture in Spiritual Formation.* Nashville: Upper Room, 2001.

Nicholi, Armand M., Jr. *The Question of God: C. S. Lewis and Sigmund Freud Debate God, Love, Sex, and the Meaning of Life.* New York: Free Press, 2002.

Norris, Kathleen. *The Cloister Walk.* New York: Riverhead, 1997.

O'Connor, D'Arcy. *The Money Pit: The Story of Oak Island and the World's Greatest Treasure Hunt.* New York: Putnam, 1978.

Rilke, Ranier Maria. *Duino Elegies and the Sonnets to Orpheus.* Translated by A. Poulin Jr. Boston: Houghton Mifflin, 1977.

Rolheiser, Ronald. *The Holy Longing: The Search for a Christian Spirituality.* New York: Doubleday, 1999.

Schaap, James C., and Abraham Kuyper. *Near unto God: Daily Meditations Adapted for Contemporary Christians.* Grand Rapids, Mich.: Eerdmans, 1997.

Schoemperlen, Diane. *Our Lady of the Lost and Found: A Novel.* New York: Penguin, 2002.

Schoenborn, Christoph. *God's Human Face: The Christ Icon.* San Francisco: Ignatius, 1994.

Shea, John. *The Hour of the Unexpected.* Allan, Tex.: Argus Communications, 1977.

Shlain, Leonard. *Art & Physics: Parallel Visions in Space, Time & Light.* New York: Quill, 1993.

Smith, Martin L. *The Word Is Very Near You: A Guide to Praying with Scripture.* Cambridge, Mass.: Cowley, 1989.

Taylor, Barbara Brown. *When God Is Silent.* Cambridge, Mass.: Cowley, 1998.

Tickle, Phyllis. *The Divine Hours: Prayers for Autumn and Wintertime.* New York: Doubleday, 2000.

Wilson, Dean. Magnolia Plantation Newsletter. Erie, Penn.: 2002.

Wullschlager, Jackie. *Hans Christian Andersen: The Life of a Storyteller.* New York: Penguin, 2000.